May wisdom
wonder
+ Love
ever awaken
in your life
+ in the lives
of all
you serve —

All ways,
Joel

To Ralph,
    always a source
of joy in my life.
            Caroline
            January 1988

*The Fine Arts of Relaxation,
Concentration and Meditation*

The Fine Arts of Relaxation, Concentration and Meditation

Ancient Skills for Modern Minds

Joel Levey

Wisdom Publications · London

First published in 1987

Wisdom Publications
23 Dering Street, London W1, England

© Joel Levey 1987

Illustrations: pp. 2, 157, 170 © Brian Beresford 1987; pp. 49,
58, 140, © Robin Bath 1987; page 69, © Albert Zeman 1987;
page 87, © Master Chuk Mor 1987; page 121, © Joseph Bailey
1987; page 214, © Moke Moketoff 1987.

British Cataloguing in Publication Data
Levey, Joel
    The fine arts of relaxation, concentration and meditation:
    ancient skills for modern minds.
    1. Relaxation
    I. Title
    613.7'9   RA785

ISBN 0 86171 040 1

Set in Palatino 10½ on 13 point by Setrite of Hong Kong, and
printed and bound by Eurasia Press of Singapore on 80 gsm
cream Sunningdale Opaque paper supplied by Link
Publishing Papers of West Byfleet, Surrey.

To my many kind teachers
and to the awakening of wisdom
within us all.

Contents

8   *The fine arts of relaxation, concentration and meditation*

Foreword

In his beautiful little book, *The Fine Arts of Relaxation, Concentration and Meditation*, Joel Levey condenses two decades of study, experience and teaching in the art of self mastery. He makes it clear that it is not stress itself that kills us, but our reaction to it, and leads the student from simple self regulation of stress responses to the heights of self knowledge, spiritual and transpersonal awareness. Hopefully everyone who reads this book will make room in their life for the practices and growth program it illustrates.

DR. ELMER GREEN
Director of the
Voluntary Controls Program
Menninger Foundation, USA

The challenge

The greatest revolution in our generation is the
discovery that human beings by changing the inner
attitudes of their minds can change
the outer aspects of their lives.
William James

As the pace of modern life continues to accelerate, skills in the fine arts of relaxation, concentration and meditation are being recognized as vital to our peace of mind, emotional well-being, health and performance. Generally speaking, most of us do not bring much attention to our bodies or minds unless we are experiencing extreme pleasure or discomfort. We are simply too caught up in the countless external and mental distractions to notice and attend to the subtle warning signs of distress. All too often we wait until the whispers of tension in our bodies, our relationships and our world have become screams of pain before we attempt to restore harmony and balance.

Though our bodies are really not very different from those of our ancestors, the world we live in is dramatically different. In a single day we may be called on to process more information and make more decisions than one of our ancestors faced in years. Given the accelerating rate of change, the immensity of personal and world problems, the pervasive anxiety, and the staggering variety of choices and decisions that are a part of our daily life it is no wonder that we often feel overwhelmed, frustrated, or as though we were missing something of vital importance in our lives.

As a society we have developed many tools to improve life, we have made quantum leaps in our technology and in our ability to manipulate the external environment. We have learned to drive cars and navigate space craft, to harness the power of the sun, wind and electricity, to communicate across the micro and macro dimensions of the universe. But how much time and money have we spent on mapping and mastering the powers of our inner worlds? And how successful have we been in creating a world in which we can live in health, happiness and harmony?

We don't understand the operations of our minds and hence don't operate them very well.
Charles Tart

In fact it is our mindbody that guides our creation and use of all these other tools, and our mindbody that is an instrument of infinite potential. Yet few of us have ever learned even the most basic skills for it's maintenance and fine tuning. Consider, did your parents or teachers teach you relaxation, concentration and meditation skills? Did they themselves practise such arts or even know of their value? Most likely not. Impoverished by a lack of such basic human skills, we in modern times have much to learn from the ancient arts and sciences of mind, and with so many people in our society suffering and even dying of stress-related diseases, it is no wonder that we have begun to look for practical alternatives to our present lifestyles.

What we are seeking is to become more fully and wholly alive. Certainly each of us will have fond memories of having experienced such quintessential moments. Most likely these came unexpectedly in the midst of ordinary activities. The spontaneous infusion of beauty and wonder that filled you one sunset...the healing serentiy and deep relaxation of dozing in the sun by a stream...the effortless flow of attention that accompanied you through some task ...the intimate sense of tenderness, love and belonging that welled up within you some moment while alone with nature or holding your child or loved one. There are a myriad of magical moments that allow us to feel and know life more deeply, but having experienced such moments of grace, most of us long to recapture them without knowing how. They remain as memories, glimpses of a state of mind beyond the familiar mode of being we experience on a daily basis.

The pages that follow contain guidelines and practical skills for becoming whole and alive. Properly used, such skills are powerful and effective methods for releasing stress and tension, understanding the nature of the mind, and enhancing the quality of life. This manual is designed as an introduction to mental fitness skills, and since it is our minds that perceive, interpret and choose our responses to the outer and inner world, these skills are of utmost importance. For simplicity the techniques have been organized into three categories: relaxation, concentration and meditation.

By mastering the *fine art of relaxation*, we learn to recognize and reduce unnecessary tension. By learning to free ourselves from this accumulated tension, we are able to reduce our discomfort, increase our efficiency, and enhance our comfort, and overall well-being.

The *fine art of concentration* teaches us how to harness the power of the mind that is ordinarily distracted and diffuse. By harnessing the mind, we are able to focus and concentrate our attention wholeheartedly upon whatever we are doing. Free from the usual whirlwind of distraction and confusion, the mind becomes a stable and powerful tool that we can use to penetrate to deeper levels of meaning and understanding.

The *fine art of meditation* reveals a myriad of ways for using every activity of our lives as a means of transforming and developing our mind. Having achieved a relaxed body and stable concentration, we can use meditation techniques to gain access to a broader spectrum of creative possibilities for seeing ourselves and responding to the world. Meditation gives us the means to reduce our negativity and enhance the positive potentials of the mind such as wisdom, power and loving kindness.

A fourth section gives some additional ideas and strategies for mental fitness.

Relaxation and beyond

This book is for everyone interested in learning methods to master stress and enhance the quality of their life. It is also a handbook for those who wish to understand and master such skills in order to teach them to others. Whatever your motivation, you will find that the ideas and techniques in this collection have been presented with an emphasis on practical application in our modern lives, whilst preserving a sense of the depth and sacredness of such inner arts of mental development. I suggest that you consider these ideas with your mind, sense their meaning for you in your heart, and test and confirm the power and practicality of these skills with your experience.

Though you begin to practice relaxation, concentration and meditation to cure your physical woes, handle your stress, or ease pain, you may find that the benefits are much greater and more far-reaching than you initially assumed. For many people, these techniques are like wish-fulfilling jewels – used properly and purposefully, they can be extremely effective in helping you to develop the latent qualities that you most wish to mature.

If you are primarily interested in physical relaxation, mental calm or clarity, you will find many of these techniques effective. If you are inclined to investigate the deep and subtle mechanisms of your bodymind, proper practice of these methods will ripen this understanding. And if you approach your practice with a heartfelt sense of devotion, a sincere yearning to deepen your spiritual understanding and be better equipped to help others effectively, many of these methods may serve as a vehicle to transform your mind and open up dimensions of your understanding where such growth can be nurtured and brought to wholeness.

Man has always known; he has known that life is fundamentally good, that the universe, the stars in the sky, the animals, plants, minerals, the elements of earth are not malevolent, but cosmically saturated with the purpose that gives order.
The purpose is the inherent sacredness, the order of the universe itself. As long as man has kept this sacredness before him, indeed, as long as he has woven it into the pattern of his heart through humility and spiritual attunement, the pattern of human society has also reflected the sacredness and order with which all things are endowed.

Jose Arguelles

Origins

This book is a distillation of over a hundred methods that I have found personally and professionally effective over the past nineteen years. During that time, I have had the rare opportunity to study and work closely with accomplished and respected masters and researchers of the inner arts and sciences. From these remarkable men and women I have learned many ancient methods of mental development that have been cherished, preserved and passed on to benefit people in modern times. The contemporary renaissance of interest in matters of spirit, consciousness, mental health and fitness has brought these methods of relaxation, concentration and meditation out of the caves, monasteries and remote cultures and into the research institutions and mainstream of our modern lives. In recent years, many of these methods of mental development have been scientifically studied and certified as being effective antidotes to the epidemic of stress-related diseases, anxiety, hostility and existential yearning that plagues our rapidly changing world.

Over the years I have used these methods as primary tools in my work as: a mental fitness coach for athletes and corporate peak performers; a researcher into the nature of human consciousness; a biofeedback clinician teaching psychophysical self regulation skills; a stress mastery and creativity consultant to mainstream business; a faculty member in graduate programs in psychology of consciousness, wholistic health and medicine; a biocybernaut instructor for a pioneering program with an elite team of US Army Special Forces troops; a counsellor for people facing terminal illness or grieving the loss of a loved one; a guide and friend to many people seeking to develop a greater sense of well-being and meaning in their lives.

Acknowledgements

The interest, enthusiasm and devoted work of many fine people have brought this book into print. The tremendous patience, presence, dreamsharing, editing, ad infinitum of my wife Michelle have nurtured and supported this book (and this author) through many stages of development. The contributions of my partners at SportsMind Inc. have been invaluable: Jacque Nugent typed the first official edition; Paul Ackerman for diagrams and author's photo; and test training of the material by Bud Cook, Chris Majer, Larry Burback and Horst Abraham. The kind offer of Caroline Wareham to edit the material was instrumental in bringing a unified cohesiveness to the manuscript which was then typed by Mary O'Malley with the help of Douglas Anderson. At that stage Pam Cowen and Steve Miller passed the manuscript on to Nick Ribush at Wisdom Publications where Lynn McDaid and later Robina Courtin with the help of Sarah Thresher and Susan Isaacs completed the editing and design work.

On an inner level, the profound depth of wisdom, ethical impeccability and compassionate activity of my teachers Kyabje Zong Rinpoche, Venerable Kalu Rinpoche, His Holiness Tenzin Gyatso the Dalai Lama, Lama Thubten Yeshe, Rina Sircar, Geshe Rabten and Chagdud Rinpoche has inspired and in countless ways contributed to this book. The inspiration of their living examples, their methods of teaching and their careful guidance of my own practice of these inner arts has deeply touched my heart and opened my mind to new dimensions of understanding.

Inspiration for this book has also come from His Holiness the Karmapa, Lama Govinda, Geshe Dhargye, Dezhung Rinpoche, Geshe Tsultrim Gyeltsen, Zasep Rinpoche, Brother David Steindle-Rast, Soen Sa Nim, Geshe Sopa, Rabbi Shlomo Carlbach, Lama Thubten Zopa, Taungpulu Sayadaw, Luding Khen Rinpoche, Dagchen Rinpoche, Ganden Tri Rinpoche, Rabbi Zalman Shachter, Pir Vilayat Khan, Reshad Field, Dhyani Ywahoo, Genki Roshi, Sasaki Roshi, Derald Langham, Jose Arguelles, Gregory Bateson and many others with whom I have studied.

Holding lineages of teachings that have been cherished and preserved for millenia, these teachers have conveyed a living transmission of ancient wisdom into modern times. In recent years many of these remarkable teachers have died. If in some way this book contributes to the continued understanding and practice of the wisdom and altruistic concern that they so inspiringly embodied and taught, my intentions will be fulfilled.

The friendship and skilful teaching styles of Alan Wallace, Ram Dass, Stephen Levine, Zasep Rinpoche, Chokyi Nyima, Jonathan Landaw, Joseph Goldstein, Jack Kornfield, Bill Arnesen, Jack Schwartz, Robert Hover, Ruth Denison, Sogyal Rinpoche, Ole Nydahl, Paul Reps, Lester Femhi and Virginia Veach have all inspired and energized aspects of my own teaching style of these skills over the years.

Also to thank for their encouragement in developing this material are Elmer and Alyce Green, Richard Strozzi-Heckler, Norm Shealy, Jean Chapman, Art Gladman, Norma Estrada, Kent Peterson, Karen Malik and many other friends and colleagues from the Council Grove Conference over the last decade; Anna Cox, Linda Dow, Shirley Begley, Robert Carlson and Alan Millar; the many members of our Tuesday evening meditation group; the many students, patients and participants in seminars whose insights have provided invaluable feedback for how these methods apply to our daily lives.

My heartfelt thanks to: Earth view Inc. for permission to

adapt numerous tracks from my compact disk 'The Fine Art of Relaxation'; Taungpulu Sayadaw and Rina Sircar for permission to include the 'Concentration while walking' exercise; Kalu Rinpoche for inspiration for the 'Spheres of mind' technique; Sogyal Rinpoche for inspiring the 'Antidote to discouragement' technique; Deborah Rozman (*Meditating with Children*, University of the Trees Press) for inspiration for the introduction to the *Concentration* section; Wisdom Publications for permission to modify 'Finding a teacher' from *How to Meditate* by Kathleen McDonald; Joseph Goldstein, Jack Kornfield, Stephen Levine and Ram Dass whose numerous quotes, inspirations and writings have contributed significantly to the content and style of this book particularly in the mindfulness meditations and the section on transforming pain; Michelle Levey for the 'Kitchen yogi meditation'; John Blofeld for the 'Mother of Compassion' meditation; Roger Walsh for the inspiration for 'A meditation for peace and action'; Alan Wallace for permission to adapt the 'Loving kindness meditation'; Tenzin Gyatso, His Holiness the Dalai Lama for permission to include his meditation on compassion; Lama Thubten Yeshe and Wisdom Publications for permission to adapt the 'Meditation on the teacher' from *Silent Mind, Holy Mind;* Joy Carey with whom I co-authored 'Strategies for mastering stress'; Michael Murphy and Stephen Donovan of the Esalen Foundation Transformation Project for allowing me to include their excellent 'Summary of contemporary meditation research.'

The quotes in this collection have come from many sources including: Marianne Anderson & Louis Savary, *Passages: A Guide to Pilgrims of the Mind,* (New York: Harper & Row, 1972). Jose Arguelles, *Earth Ascending,* (Boston: Shambhala, 1984). Garma C.C. Chang, *Buddhist Teachings on Totality,* (London: P.S.U.P., 1977); Fritjof Capra, *Tao of Physics,* (Boulder: Shambhala, 1975); Carlos Castenada, *Tales of Power,* (New York: Simon & Schuster, 1974); Larry Dossey, *Time, Space and Medicine,* (Boston: Shambhala, 1982); Ram Dass,

Journey of Awakening, (New York: Bantam, 1978); Joseph Goldstein, *The Experience of Insight,* (Boston: Shambhala, 1986); Jack Kornfield, *Living Buddhist Masters,* (Santa Cruz: Unity Press, 1977); Jean Millay, 'Brainwave Correlates of Psi,' *Psi Research.* 2:1, 1983: Institute of Noetic Sciences Newsletters; Hanuman Foundation Newsletters; Inquiring Mind Newsletters. Quotes for the 'Sports: a Western yoga' section were drawn from: Charles Garfield *Peak Performance Strategies & Insights of America's Most Productive People* (Morrow, 1986). Charles Garfield & Hal Bennett, *Peak Performance: Mental Training Techniques of the World's Greatest Athletes,* (L.A.: Tarcher, 1984). Michael Murphy and Rhea White, *The Psychic Side of Sports,* (London: Addison Wesley, 1978); Bill Bradley, *Life on the Run,* (New York: Time Books, 1976); W.B. Furlong, 'The Flow Experience: The Fun in Fun,' *Psychology Today,* June 1976; Daniel Goleman, 'Meditation and Consciousness: An Asian Approach to Mental Health'. *American Journal of Psychotherapy,* 30 (1975): 41 – 54; W.P. Morgan, 'Test of Champions,' *Psychology Today,* 14:2 (1980): 92 – 102; Michael Novak, *Joy of Sports,* (New York: Basic Books, 1976); Carl Powers, *Psychophysiological Effects of Biofeedback, Open Focus Self Regulation Training Upon Homeostatic Efficiency During Exercise,* doctoral dissertation, (Dept. of Movement Science & Physical Education, Florida University, 1980).

I would also like to thank my first teachers: my grandparents Hilda and Abe Levey, whose faith, humour and kindness inspired me to value what I do; and my mother, Recia Millar, whose determination to live was my first example of the power of faith, prayer and devotion.

It has been through the wisdom and kindness of these and countless others that my confusions have been clarified, my insights confirmed and these many methods of developing the potentials of the mind have become a part of my life. May they now become a part of yours.

How to get the most from this book

There are many thousands of techniques for developing relaxation, concentration and meditation. Each of these is effective for enhancing particular strengths and reducing certain weaknesses in order to fully develop the potentials of the human mindbody. In this book I have selected those that I have found to be most widely effective, though it is for each reader to find the ideas and methods best suited to their own needs.

Mastery of these techniques comes in three ways. *Reading or hearing* the methods is the first step. *Contemplating and thinking* about their meaning and application in ordinary life is the second step. *Deeply settling into the experience of each technique* is the third step and the key to actualizing its potential in your life. Do not expect instant results. Though some benefit may quickly become apparent, the real benefit of any of these methods will be gradual and come from frequent practice. How long will it take you to master a technique? How long would it take you to learn to master the flute or cello? The key to all learning is a personal commitment and discipline.

The book is arranged in four sections: *Relaxation, Concentration, Meditation*, and *More strategies for mental fitness*. Each of the first three sections has an introduction to the primary ideas and methods, a description of the basic guidelines for using these methods and then the methods themselves.

I would suggest that you read the introduction and guidelines for each section carefully before reading through the techniques themselves. Note those that you intuitively sense will work for you. Once you have identified them, put them into practice by reading them slowly and thoughtfully, and then proceeding step by step to get the feeling behind the words. You may find it helpful to have a friend read the exercise to you, or to record it in your own voice on a cassette recorder to replay at your leisure. Or you may feel inspired to change my terminology to better suit your style or belief. As you become more familiar with a technique you will know how to mentally guide yourself through its stages without needing to read or listen to the instructions. Though at first you may mentally talk yourself through an exercise, gradually cultivate the skill to move through the exercise as a series of mental images or feelings instead of conceptual words and ideas.

Part One
Relaxation

Do everything with a mind that lets go.
Do not expect any praise or reward.
If you let go a little, you will have a little peace.
If you let go a lot, you will have a lot of peace.
If you let go completely, you will know complete
peace and freedom.
Your struggles with the world
will have come to an end.

Achaan Chah

Dynamic relaxation

The relaxation described in the pages that follow is not a passive, limp or ineffective state, but one characterized by a dynamic, ever adapting balance of arousal and relaxation, finely tuned to meet the ever changing demands of daily life. With practice you will learn to immediately feel when you are holding more tension than you need to perform at your best. By learning to release the tension that you don't need, your brain and muscles will be vitalized with oxygen and nutrients, you will be able to think more clearly and make better decisions, and your ability to act will be enhanced.

Relaxation skills are the foundation for practicing concentration and meditation. You probably know from experience how difficult it is to harness and focus the power of your mind when your body is filled with tension and your mind clouded by fatigue and anxiety.

Once you begin to understand and practice the skills described here, the tensions and distress of your life can be met as opportunities to apply and refine your growing skills in relaxation. This requires the conscious cultivation of:

1. Self awareness: the ability to know what you are experiencing — sensing, feeling, thinking, etc — at any moment.
2. Care and kindness: the authentic and heartfelt concern that deliberately chooses the paths that lead to greater harmony in your mental, physical, and personal relationships with the world.

3. A joyful appreciation of the process: an attitude of gratitude and openness to learning and growing from life's
unceasing challenges. A joyful dedication to living a
game to be mastered in the arena of your own mindbody
and relationships.

4. Commitment and courage: the willingness to do whatever it takes to continue to realize and nurture your own
extraordinary potentials and help others do the same.

Relaxation skills build the foundation for your practice of
concentration and meditation. They allow you to release the
accumulated tension and pass along the continuum of
health and performance pictured below. This is a dynamic
process, leaving us at times immobilized by distress, at
times simply coping with our tensions and anxieties, and at
times energized, calm and confident, having all the informa-

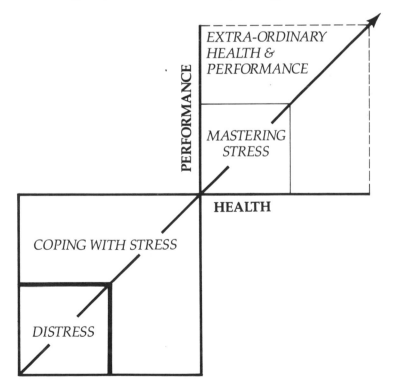

tion and ability we need to master the stressful demands that life's changing conditions inevitably bring.

Though stress and tension will always be a part of your life, when you know how to relax, there is no need to get tense about being tense, or feel anxious about feeling anxious. Stress will energize rather than destroy you. Change and challenge will provide every opportunity for growth, creative expression and extraordinary levels of health, performance and insight.

As you learn to reduce the noise in your system, physical vitality, mental clarity, calm, centered strength and emotional well-being will naturally and effortlessly arise.

With this in mind, let's look at the guidelines and methods of practicing the fine arts of relaxation.

Remember...
Relaxation is not something that you do.
It is a natural response that you allow to happen.
Relaxation is what is left when you stop creating
tension.

Guidelines for developing relaxation skills

1. *Motivation*

When you start to practice relaxation or mental development skills it is important to understand why you are doing it and to generate a positive motivation towards this learning process. *Choose* to practice relaxation, do not practice under pressure from others. Remember that it is not what you do but how and why you do it that matters.

2. *Regular practice*

Make these relaxation tools work for you. Regular, consistent practice is essential if you want to gain maximum benefit from these skills. Remember that when you learn to, say, ride a bicycle, develop marksmanship or any other physical skill you are using muscles you have never used before. So too when you learn how to relax: you will be stretching mental muscles that you have never been aware of before.

Many people recommend that you practice twenty minutes in the morning and twenty minutes in the evening — this would be excellent. Also, you could practice an additional forty minutes each day — a minute here, five minutes there, standing in line, waiting on the telephone, pausing for a few breaths at a stop light. Gradually these skills will become programmed into your biocomputer and be easily and dependably accessible to you whenever you need them.

3. *A quiet environment*

It is better at first to practice in quiet, comfortable surroundings. This will help you to zero in on the physical and mental qualities you are learning to develop.

Once you have become familiar with your internal controls, and how to access your target state, you will be able to carry your practice over into more stressful environments. In fact, the world will continually provide you with opportunities to test and refine your skills in the face of challenge and the unexpected. Having mastered these skills, it is possible that at some critical moment, when it really counts, you will have the energy, balance and clarity to touch somebody's life in a meaningful way — and this includes your own.

4. *Focusing the mind*

At the beginning of each session, it is helpful to employ a concentration technique (see pp.65–86) such as watching the breath, repeating a word or phrase, or contemplating an internal image or quality. This phase of the session helps you bring the mind into focus, energizing concentration and reducing mental agitation and distraction. Once concentration has been established, it can be directed towards any object or goal unwaveringly.

5. *Effortlessness and voluntary surrender*

This state is characterized by an alert, receptive and calm intensity of awareness. Initially, the challenge is to learn to develop a fine balance between an open, calm attentiveness and the more tightly focused mind that tries to change something or make something happen. This balance is learned through practice and attention to the feedback you receive from your attempts to relax your body and mind.

For best results, *allow relaxation to happen*. The harder you try, the tenser you will become. Release your tensions as you exhale. Relax into the gentle pull of gravity. Let your eyes be soft. In an easy, natural and effortless manner, just let go of the mindbody tensions that you no longer need. Allow your internal RPMs to slow down and find your natural rhythm.

If you are the type of person who has always been busy doing rather than being, this approach may at first be alien to you. With practice, however, you will discover a totally new type of inner strength and power when you are deeply relaxed. Don't worry about losing control. Whenever you need to apply effort or push harder you will be rested enough to do so. You are simply learning to have the choice of two operating modes rather than the compulsive limitation of one inefficient habit. Without this option you may struggle for the rest of your life to keep control rather than simply settling into the power of life, naturally and effortlessly.

6. *Proper posture*

For best results, a comfortable upright position is recommended for practicing these relaxation techniques. It is important that your spine is straight. Lying down is discouraged if you have a tendency to fall asleep. With practice, you will find that you can tune in to an optimal balance between relaxation and activation while walking, talking, driving or engaging in any activity.

7. *External guidance, internal guidance*

Initially, the external guidance of another person or a taped guided relaxation is useful as it is easier to just let go into the experience. As you become familiar with the stages of relaxation and the variety of mental and physical indicators, you will be able to enter these states at will and under your own guidance. The balance that you develop is similar to simultaneously driving a car and being free to enjoy the view, or playing music and being totally entranced by it at the same time.

For most of us, this is an unfamiliar state of awareness. With practice, however, you will expand your mental and physical awareness to allow you to easily guide your own relaxation sessions.

8. *Timing*

Once you have become familiar with the relaxation techniques by practicing morning and evening, you will be able to apply them when you need to throughout the day as an antidote to stressful situations. You may wonder, however, just when the best time would be to actually apply them. Generally speaking, it is best to practice *before* you are mentally or physically exhausted. And do not practice on a full stomach or when you are extremely hungry.

If you wait until you just can't take any more, odds are your mind will be so agitated that it will be almost impossible to concentrate. And if you wait until you are exhausted or full from eating, you will probably fall asleep. As in a leaky boat — remember you have a bilge pump. Don't wait until you feel swamped or out of control.

Remember that your bodymind is your primary instrument. Monitor it carefully throughout the day. Consciously relax or fine-tune frequently.

If you are having difficulty settling down and tuning in, try scheduling your relaxation sessions immediately after periods of exercise or heightened arousal. At these times there is a tangible mental and physical release, a natural time of letting go. Just ride the wave of this shift from sympathetic nervous system activation to the parasympathetic relaxation response. At this time investigate and recognize the stages, feelings and indicators of relaxation while they are most apparent.

9. *Overcoming difficulties*

There are two main obstacles that you will inevitably encounter in your practice — distraction and drowsiness.

Distraction is of two types: external, such as noise, heat, cold, etc. and internal, such as physical sensations, pain, and mental wandering. The best strategy in both cases is to include the distraction in your awareness while minimizing your resistance to or identification with the distracting event. Just let it be, and keep your attention on what you are doing. Even if your mind wanders a thousand times, gently bring it back. Do not engage in mental commentary on the process − just do it. Gradually, the agitated, wandering mind will be tamed and you will be able to stay focused on the task at hand.

As for *drowsiness* or mental dullness, it would be useful to check your posture to make sure you are sitting upright. You could take a few deep breaths, or even splash your face with cold water before continuing your practice. If you are practicing outside, you could sit, say, close to the edge of a cliff or in a place where you need to be alert.

You might find it helpful to contemplate the preciousness of your life and the unpredictability of your death, and to muster a firm resolve to make the most of each moment.

Don't allow your wandering, compulsive mind to control your life, and likewise, don't wait to wake up on your death-bed realizing that you have slept through most of your life. *Take charge! Be patient!*

10. *Choosing a technique*

As we begin our practice of these skills, our challenge is to recognize and to master our stress response. Since each of us has a unique style of responding to the stressors of our daily life, different techniques geared to optimize psychophysical states will be effective for different individuals. For example, if your symptoms of stress include neuromuscular signs such as muscle aches and pain, tension headaches, back-aches, spasms or tics, fatigue etc., then the methods of modified progressive relaxation, autogenic imagery, the flow sequence, mental massage and numerous other methods may be quite effective.

If your symptoms of distress are primarily cognitive such as anxiety, worry, intrusive or repetitive thoughts, etc. then the concentration techniques and the meditations for listening, walking, investigating the mind and thought may be very helpful.

If your symptoms include autonomic nervous system symptoms or disease including hypertension, migraines, gastrointestinal distress, poor circulation, excessive sweating, eating disorders, etc. you might benefit from consistent practice of autogenic imagery, hollow body meditation and the practices of giving and taking, loving kindness and forgiveness.

If you are prone to negative and unsettling emotions such as anger, impatience, guilt, obsessive desire, etc. then the concentration techniques may offer temporary relief while the meditations on the mind, thoughts, forgiveness, loving kindness, compassion and the practice of giving and taking may help to uproot the deeper causes of your emotional distress.

Individuals suffering from chronic pain may find some relief from the practice of relaxation techniques in general followed by the use of mental massage, hollow body, and the strategies for transforming pain.

If you feel that you have mastered your response to life's myriad stressors and that your wish is to tap your latent potentials, virtually every method described in this book holds the potential to open new horizons of understanding, performance and humankindness.

11. *Release phenomena*

As you begin to relax, it is quite common to experience what are called 'release phenomena.' Some of these are jerking or quivering of the body as when one falls asleep, gurgling of the stomach, tingling feelings or numbness, perspiration, memories or feelings or perceptual changes spontaneously arising. Remember that it is natural to become aware of certain experiences when we are relaxed that we wouldn't normally notice during times of activity. For example, you may be injured while playing a game but because of the excitment you do not notice the pain until later when you have slowed down.

Release phenomena are common indicators that your practice of relaxation or meditation techniques is becoming effective in dissolving your mental, emotional and physical tension. The best way to deal with these experiences as they occur is to regard them without judgement — you may find them either disturbing or quite pleasant. Simply allow them to arise, flow freely and dissolve without distracting your attention.

Most of us are more familiar with the signs of stress than with the indicators of relaxation. With practice, you will become aware of the subtle physical, emotional and mental states associated with progressively deeper levels of relaxation and meditation. Eventually, your reservoirs of stress will be drained and your circuits cleared, allowing you to handle the challenges of daily life more effectively and with greater patience and understanding. When you are on the right track, a sigh, a tingling, a sense of deep warmth will become a familiar signpost on your daily stroll through your inner landscape.

12. *Inner and outer discipline*

The success of your relaxation and meditation program is directly related to your discipline in your relationship to the world. Plagued as we usually are by anger, fear, jealousy, guilt or worry, it is extremely difficult to develop the concentration and understanding necessary to master our minds. The conflicts of our day to day lives will become painfully clear to us the moment we focus our attention within in our practice. Ignoring these conflicts doesn't make them go away. Instead, we are faced with the challenge of truly mastering our lives rather than being a slave to our mental distortions and emotional confusions.

As you exercise more discipline in your relationship to the world, your ability to concentrate and focus the mind will grow. With this enhanced mental clarity and stability, new understanding and insight will reveal better approaches to living. Thus, inner and outer discipline reinforce each other.

13. *Alterations in consciousness*

> *A human being is a part of the whole called by us*
> *'universe,' a part limited in time and space. He*
> *experiences himself, his thoughts and feelings as*
> *something separate from the rest. A kind of optical*
> *delusion of consciousness. This delusion is a kind of*
> *prison for us, restricting us to our personal desires*
> *and to affection for a few persons nearest to us. Our*
> *task must be to free ourselves from the prison by*
> *widening our circle of compassion to embrace all*
> *living creatures and the whole of nature in its beauty.*
> Albert Einstein

It would seem that all of us suffer from 'an optical delusion of consciousness.' Each of us has been hypnotized from birth to perceive and interpret both internal and external events in a very limited way. Each culture has its own brand of cultural hypnosis that conditions its members to attend to certain aspects of reality and to virtually ignore others. For instance, the Eskimos have many words for snow, the Tibetans describe at least eighty-five states of consciousness, and some cultures believe that their dream worlds are more real than their ordinary waking experiences.

Many of the techniques in this book are actually methods for de-conditioning, ways of relaxing the limitations of our view of who we are, how we perform and what is happening in the world around us. All the techniques here can be included in two categories. *Concentrative* techniques help us to focus our attention, and *receptive* techniques help us to scan the full spectrum of the world in a wide open way. In fact, the complete picture is being broadcast to us on many tracks simultaneously, but for most of our life we have been monitoring only one of these tracks at a time.

During moments of peak performance, relaxation, dreams, intuition, physical exercise, meditation, sexual experience or prayer, the spectrum of our awareness may expand to incorporate new ways of experiencing and knowing – so-called, altered states of consciousness (ASC). Psychologist Dr. William James sums up the challenge of integrating a full spectrum of awareness into our daily lives:

> *Our normal waking consciousness, rational consciousness as we call it, is but one special type of consciousness, whilst all about it parted by the flimsiest of screens, there lie potential forms of consciousness entirely different. We may go through life without suspecting their existence: but apply the requisite stimuli and at a touch they are there in all their completeness, definite types of mentality, which probably somewhere have their field of adaptation. No account of the universe in its totality can be final, which leaves other forms of consciousness quite disregarded. How to regard them is the question – for they are so discontinuous with ordinary consciousness. Yet they may determine attitudes though they cannot furnish formulas and open a region though they fail to give a map. At any rate, they forbid a premature closing of our accounts of reality.*

14. Dynamic action

Would you spend hours cooking a meal and then rush out without eating it? If you practice the techniques here and then leap up and compulsively dive into unconscious activity, you have missed the point. Relaxation and meditation sessions are times to focus your mind, fine-tune your energies and prepare for dynamic and effective action. It is the time that allows you to be out on the spinning rim of life and still feel the stillness, power and calm at the centre of your being.

As you end a session, consciously carry that energy into action. Throughout the day, frequently scan your circuits, fine-tune as necessary, and demonstrate the effectiveness of the skills you have been working so hard to master.

15. *The five powers*

The five mental powers that are essential for developing mental fitness are (1) confidence/trust, (2) energy, (3) concentration, (4) mindfulness/attention, and (5) insight/understanding. They are effective antidotes to the five hindrances of (1) doubt/fear, (2) lethargy/procrastination, (3) distraction/ agitation, (4) forgetfulness and (5) confusion.

Would you ever begin anything if you lacked even the basic confidence in your ability to accomplish it or at least to learn from the experience? A sense of confidence is essential if your practice of the fine arts of relaxation, concentration and meditation are to have results. The sense of trust and *confidence* counteracts your *doubts* and helps you transform

every experience gained during your practice into grist for the mill of your insight and growth.

Hope and fear, pain and ecstasy; every moment of change and flow reveals to you the nature of your mind and body. This understanding can set you free from old emergency reactions and compulsive behavior.

Understanding of process enables a person to gain control of that process or to gain freedom from being controlled by it. Thus, analytic understanding of the atomic components of blind rage — what triggers it, how it directs itself, how it mobilized mental, verbal and physical energies and so on enables an habitually angry person to begin to control his or her temper, perhaps finally to become free of its control.
The Dalai Lama

Though you may have little control over the specific contents of your thoughts, images and feelings, you will discover that you have the power to alter the process through which you relate to the contents of your mind.

Beginning your practice with a joyful mind and a sense of confidence will help you to tap the second power, *energy*. It will help you overcome the hindrance of *lethargy* or *procrastination* and will move you along on the spiral of growth.

Having generated the powers of confidence and energy, they must be blended with the powers of *concentration* and *mindfulness*. Concentration provides a focus and the clarity to direct the energy of your intention. Mindfulness is the quality of attention that allows you to remember what you are doing. Concentration counteracts *distraction* and dullness, and mindfulness is the antidote to forgetting what you are doing.

Understanding that your initial beliefs, calculations or intuitions were valid or having gained insight into how they must be modified, the power of your self confidence will naturally grow. Your understanding will overpower the immobilizing obstacles of your doubt and fear. This power of confidence based on previous success and understanding can then serve to propel you on through a spiralling growth curve of heightened energy, concentration, mindfulness and wisdom.

Having maintained your initial intention through the powers of confidence, energy, concentration and mindfulness, the fifth power of *insight* will naturally and effortlessly ripen. The disciplined mind will have the integrity to reach deep and sometimes profound insights regarding this remarkable process called yourself.

The following compendium of relaxation techniques is intended to familiarize you with a variety of skills and strategies. Read through and choose those that seem to speak most directly to your own needs and interests. Feel free to adapt any words or images to your own style. With practice you will become familiar with the unique characteristics and indicators of each of these techniques and you will be able to recommend or teach appropriate ones to others.

Bring a joyful mind to your practice of these skills. Remember how short and tenuous your life really is.

1 Letting go of tension

This technique will help you to recognize the various levels of tension that you experience throughout the day, and will help you to relax.

First, tense your whole body as tightly as possible. Clench your fists, flex your feet and toes. Make a face — squeeze tightly but not so tightly that you hurt yourself. Squeeze... tense...and hold for a few moments. Notice what it feels like to be this tense. Hold...and now relax, relax completely ...allow your beath to fill you naturally, and as you exhale, let go completely. Let go into gravity. Release any tensions that you don't need. Allow the waves of breath to ebb and flow.

Now, once again, tense your whole body, but this time tense only half as much as before. Tense...hold...feel what it is like to hold this level of tension. Hold...and let go. As you breathe, let go completely of any tensions in your mind and body. Allow each breath to carry away all your tension. Now, feel what it is like to have released and let go of tension.

Once again, tense your whole body, but again only half as much as the last time. Tense...hold...feel how it is to have this level of tension in your body. Feel the bracing, squeezing, holding. Recognize that frequently throughout the day you are probably as tense as this without knowing it. Now, exhale...let go completely. Allow the waves of breath to wash away the tension. Let go into gravity. Feel your body opening to the flow of life. Feel your vitality and a deep, pervasive warmth within you.

Again, tense your body, and again, only half as much as the time before. Scan your body and feel the subtle ways in which tension pervades it. Hold...feel it...and let go completely. Gently relax into the flow of your breath. Allow your body and mind to find their perfect harmony.

Now, tense only your mind. Clench your attention around a thought or anxiety. Hold...feel the subtle pain in your heart closing around fear, anger, doubt, guilt. Generate a wish to be free from this pain and tension. Now breathe... open...release. Allow your mind and heart to open to the flow of thoughts, images and feelings within the sphere of your experience. Rest in this openness. Watch as fear, anxiety and doubt float by. Feel the deep, quiet strength that pervades your entire being.

When you are ready, take a few deep breaths. As you breathe, consciously infuze your body with a heightened sense of vitality...infuze your mind with clarity and claim... fill your heart with warmth, tenderness and appreciation for yourself and the world you live in. Carry this feeling with you and allow it to pervade and energize your next activity.

2 *Flow sequence*

Access

Pause
Become aware of your surroundings.
Feel where your body touches the world.
Bring your awareness to the weight and warmth
where your body touches your own body.

As you breathe,
exhale long and slow,
softly sigh as though releasing a heavy load.
Let go into gravity.
Allow the inhalation to come naturally,
effortlessly receive the breath.

Scan your body for signs of tensions.
Breathe your awareness into those regions.
As you exhale, soften and open around the tension.
Smile to yourself.
Gently remind yourself.
'I don't need to hold this in my body.'

After scanning and releasing throughout your whole body,
allow *all* sensations to flow within the space of your
awareness experience the symphony of life resonating
within your body.

Remember − there is space for *all* sensations
within your experience.

If tension or pain still remain, soften around it.
Allow the sensations to float freely and to change
without resistance.
Gently bring your awareness to the flow of thoughts,
feelings and images in your mind.
Simply notice (without commentary) how they change
from moment to moment.
Attend to the *process* of change without concern
for the particular *content* of the thoughts and
images.
If you notice your attention tightening around
any thought, feeling, image or sensation, simply
notice the gripping, smile to yourself,
breathe into it, and let it *flow.*

Appreciation

Now, simply rest in the *flow.*
Remember – there is space for *everything*
within your experience.
Resistance is pain.
Trust gravity.
Relax into the *flow*...
Allow your awareness to become subtler with each breath
Appreciate the resonant quality of the flow state.
Practise fine-tuning and returning to this resonant
flow state.

Re-entry and expression

Once again, become aware of your
contact with the world around you.
With eyes closed, sense the space around you.
Sense how the surrounding space connects you to everything.
Experience the sounds, smells and feelings filling this
space.

As your eyes gently open,
  allow them to be soft and receptive.
    See without *looking.*
  Aware of breath...
    Aware of gravity...
      Aware of the resonance...
        of free flowing life within you.
          Carry the calm vitality of this
            experience into action...

Cultivation

Human circuitry is remarkably sensitive to change. It requires frequent fine-tuning to maintain peak performance.

Life will inevitably challenge you.

Monitor your stress levels throughout each day. By consciously recognizing and reducing the 'noise' in your life, an underlying harmony naturally begins to emerge.

Patient, persistent practice pays off. If you have thirty seconds at a stop light or thirty minutes at lunch or after exercise, use it to fine-tune your system. Even if some tension still remains afterwards, give yourself credit for what you let flow. We each come fully equipped with everything we need to learn how to relax. Perhaps no one has ever showed you how to access these potentials.

With practice, you will notice some wonderful changes in your body, mind and performance.

Free flow: ten simple steps for mastering stress

The following ten steps will guide you through the basic stages of the previous technique. Once you understand this basic outline you will have a simple, quick and effective stress method for recognizing and reducing symptoms of stress before they can accumulate.

1. Pause, and relax into a comfortable position with spine straight.

2. Become aware of your surroundings.
3. Breathe awareness into your body.
   Exhale long and slow,
      sighing, ahh...trust gravity.
         Allow inhalations to fill you effortlessly.
4. Scan your body for signs of tensions.
5. Smile tenderly to yourself, remembering,
   'I don't need to squeeze so tightly.'
6. Open and gently soften around any tension or pain.
7. Eyes soft, jaw relaxed, arms heavy and warm, mind at ease, rest and be energized by the release of free flowing life around you.
8. Picture in your mind your next activity and imagine carrying this feeling into action.
9. Gently open your focus to be aware of the space around you.
10. Carry this calm vitality into action.
    Experience this *free flow* at work.
       Share it with others.

3 *Relaxing the body*

1. Select a comfortable place to sit or lie down. Remove your shoes, loosen your belt or tight clothing. Stretch out on your back, arms resting by your sides, feet slightly apart, eyes gently closed.
2. Think to yourself, 'Now I am going to relax completely. When I finish I will feel fully refreshed and energized.'
3. Bring your attention to your feet, wiggle your toes, flex your ankles. Then *let go*, release all the tension, and let your feet rest limp and heavy.
4. Bring your attention to your legs, your knees and thighs, up to your hips. Imagine them just sinking into the floor or chair, heavy and relaxed.
5. Bring your attention to your arms, elbows, and upper arms, all the way up to your shoulders. Imagine all the tension just melting away.
6. Bring your attention to your abdomen. Let the tension go, and allow your breathing to flow more smoothly and deeply.
7. Bring your attention to your stomach and chest, up to your throat and neck. As you continue breathing more deeply, just imagine all the tension flowing out as you are relaxing more and more deeply.
8. Now, bring awareness to your throat, neck and head, feeling loose and relaxed. Relax your facial muscles. Let the jaw drop, parting the lips and teeth. Picture yourself completely relaxed.
9. If you are aware of any remaining tension anywhere in

the body, mentally go to that area and allow tension to release and dissolve away.

10. Continue to remain in this completely relaxed state for five to ten minutes. You may picture pleasant thoughts, or simply blank your mind and enter a state of light sleep.

11. When you are ready to get up, say to yourself, 'I have been deeply relaxed. I am now ready to awaken, feeling completely refreshed, energized and relaxed.'

12. Begin to move by flexing the ankles, wiggling the toes. Then wiggle the fingers, and gently shake your wrists.

13. Bend the right knee, and then the left knee. Bend the right arm and then the left arm.

14. Open your eyes. Stretch each arm over your head. Then slowly sit or stand up, and stretch again. You are now ready to continue with your activities.

4 Body scan

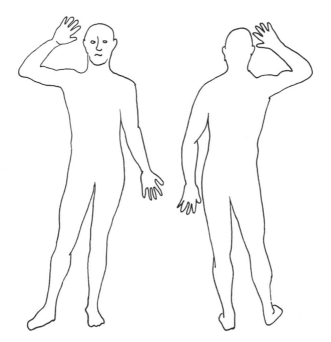

This body scan technique will help you to reclaim the all too often 'lost world' of your body. With continued use of this charting technique and frequent mental scans throughout the day, the richness of physical sensual aliveness will continue to reveal itself to you and the warning signs of stress will be quickly recognized.

Indicate intensity of sensations in any region in the illustrations above on a scale of −5 to +5, 0 being neutral, −5 extreme discomfort, and +5 extreme pleasure. Doodle in the *feelings* of tingling, vibration, density, numbness, etc. Do not draw conceptualized anatomical structures, (i.e. bones, organs, etc.). Graphically represent feelings in any region you have awareness of.

5 *Autogenic imagery*

This practice is particularly effective for bringing harmony to your mindbody. It uses a special sequence of phrases or formuli that directly affect the control systems of your body.

Begin by assuming a comfortable position. Keep your body still and comfortable. Take five slow, full breaths inhaling and exhaling through both nostrils. Then begin to breathe slowly and smoothly with no pause between exhalations and inhalations. Gently concentrate your attention on the sensations of breath flowing past the tip of your nostrils. If your mind wanders, gently bring it back to the space between the nostrils. Continue now to breathe slowly and easily without having to strain to get more air.

Images for quietening the body

Now, as you silently repeat or listen to the following phrases, effortlessly allow yourself to visualize, imagine and feel the flow of relaxation pervading your entire body. Simply allow the body to respond to these world-images:

I feel quiet...I am beginning to feel quite relaxed...my feet, my ankles, my knees and my hips feel heavy, relaxed and comfortable...the whole central region of my body feels relaxed and quiet...my hands feel heavy warm and relaxed...my arms and my shoulders feel heavy, relaxed and comfortable...my neck, my jaw, and my forehead feel deeply relaxed. They feel comfortable and smooth...my whole body feels quiet, comfortable and deeply relaxed...

Images for quietening the emotions

Continue now to remain comfortable and relaxed as you visualize, imagine and *feel* the following phrases for calming your emotions and enfuzing your body with warmth:

My arms and hands are heavy and warm...I feel quiet, very quiet...my arms and hands are relaxed, relaxed and warm...my hands are warm...warmth is flowing into my hands, they are warm...very warm...my hands are warm ...relaxed and warm...as I breath I am filled with warmth and well being...exhaling I am able to let my heart and mind open to allow my feelings to come and flow...

Images for quietening the mind

With each phrase, imagine and *feel* a growing internal quietness and heightening of internal attention:

I feel quiet now...my mind is very quiet, calm and clear... as I withdraw my thoughts from the surroundings and I feel serene, still and at ease...deep within myself I can visualize and experience myself as relaxed, comfortable, open, flowing and still...I am alert in an easy, effortless, quiet inward turned way...my mind is calm, clear and quiet... I feel an inward quality of stillness and quiet.

Energizing the mind and body

When you are ready to move into action, mentally imagine and affirm the following phrases as you stretch your body:

I feel rested and reenergized now...I can feel life energy flowing through my arms and hands...I feel life energy moving and flowing through my face, and pervading my arms, chest and abdomen, my legs and lower body...my whole body feels energized, enlivened and unified and wholey alive...my mind is calm, clear and alert...I feel alert, enlivened and ready for action.

When you're ready, stretch, breathe and allow your eyes to gently open.

6 *Creating an inner oasis*

Sit or lie comfortably and draw your attention inwards. Allow outer sounds and movements to come and go without distraction. Now, allow your inner vision to draw you to a special place of beauty, peace or power that represents an idealized environment or atmosphere for your deep relaxation and reenergizing. This may be a scene from your memory or imagination, or a composite image of both fantasy and reality. It should be a quiet environment, perhaps by the seashore, in the mountains, or even in your own backyard.

Allow this image to come alive for you now. Vividly imagine with all your senses, that you are actually here alive in this experience. As you breathe, energize all of your senses. Vividly see the shapes and colors around you. Hear the sounds in the environment around you. Smell the fragrances in the air and taste any wonderful flavors that are a part of this vision. With your body, feel the temperature of the air or breeze and sense the shapes and textures of the world around you here. And spatially sense yourself amidst your surroundings, being aware of what is above you, behind you, in front of you, and to either side.

Rest here now. Heal, harmonize and come to rest. Allow each breath to infuze you with calm, power, clarity and peacefulness — whatever feelings you most need. Allow your mind to absorb the peacefulness and natural vitality of this wonderful place. Experience or imagine your body and mind as whole and complete. Imagine and sense your bodymind coming into a perfect harmony and resonance with the healing and energizing qualities of this special place of beauty, peace and strength. Rest here now. Absorb whatever qualities or energies that you most need. Allow yourself to be attuned to a state of perfect harmony and resonance.

When you are ready, gently allow this image to melt into openness within you. Carrying with you all of the energy, vitality, beauty, power, peace, serenity and strength of this mental oasis, become aware of your surroundings. As you breathe imagine that you are receiving inspiration from this place within you. As you move into action, feel as though these positive feelings are welling up within your mind and body, and flowing into your outer life and actions. Let your outer world reflect some of the special qualities of your inner oasis.

7 Rainbow light relaxation

Begin by sitting comfortably, with your spine straight, your eyes soft, jaw loose and body relaxed.

Now vivdly imagine that you are surrounded by a luminous mist of relaxation and well-being. Mentally give this mist a red color* and a warm comforting emotional feeling. Next, begin a cycle of five deep and slow breaths. As you inhale this relaxing mist and hold the breath for a slow count of five, imagine it filling your head, neck and shoulder and soaking deeply into every pore and fiber of your head, neck and shoulders. As you breathe out, imagine exhaling all of your physical tensions, thoughts, cares, or mental dullness that may be stored in this region of your body. Imagine exhaling any physical, emotional or mental disease as smoke or fog being flushed completely out of your body by this luminous relaxing mist. Imagine this fog or smoke dissolving completely into the space around you.

With a second cycle of five breaths, focus upon your torso

*Different colors may subtly influence different effects for different people at different times. Once you have mastered the basic visualization, experiment with imagining different colors to determine what frequency of the mental spectrum works best for you. If you find it difficult to visualize colors, begin by looking at an appropriately colored piece of paper, foil or film or at a spectrum of sunlight cast on a wall by a crystal. With practice this technique will become both simple and powerfully effective.

including your hands and arms. Vividly imagine and feel this relaxing mist flowing in through your nostrils, filling the center of your chest and then spreading out throughout your hands, arms and torso, filling this region completely with a luminous, warm, relaxing feeling of red mist and light. As before, hold the first breath for a slow count of five, allowing the oxygen to saturate and nourish your tissues and wash away the waste products from your muscles and brain. Vividly imagine that this entire region is now alive with a vitalizing red glow of deep relaxation.

With a third cycle of five breaths, direct your attention to your lower body including your hips, buttocks, genitals, legs and feet. As you inhale, vividly imagine this luminous relaxing mist flowing down to your navel and as you exhale imagine it diffuzing to completely fill the whole lower portion of your body. Allow the muscles and tissues to be oxygenated and cleansed. Allow the following breaths to find their own natural rhythms and depth. Vividly sense and imagine this entire region of your body aglow with a deep soothing sense of relaxation, warmth and vitality.

With a last cycle of five breaths, vividly imagine that you are breathing in a pure crystaline mist and rainbow-like light. Allow the waves of the breath to come and flow effortlessly at their own natural rhythm. Imagine that this luminous substance flows first to the center of your chest and then pours forth throughout your whole body. Direct this powerful purifying and harmonizing light to any region of your body that is out of balance and which calls for healing. Sense and deeply feel that your whole being is now pure and clear like a crystal body which is flooded by rainbow light. Like brilliant light pouring through a crystal imagine this luminous energy pouring through you and out into the world. Imagine that as you mentally direct it to others this light helps to dissolve their tensions, calm their minds and open their hearts to a greater sense of relaxation, warmth and well-being. Vividly sense and affirm that this energy and light that pours through you brings greater harmony to the world in which you live. This becomes a very simple, very quiet yet powerful gift or blessing that you offer to the world.

You will find that the more vivid your multi-sensory imagery, the more powerful and effective will be your use of visualization techniques on your own mindbody, on the minds and bodies of others and on the world in which you live. If it is difficult for you to imagine seeing and feeling the colors and mist, energize your practice with a strong sense of confidence and conviction that it is happening all the same. As you become familiar with this basic technique, energize and enhance your practice by giving the luminous mist a soothing fragrance, a pleasing sound, and even a soothing or pleasing taste.

Once you are familiar with this basic technique, you will be able to access the same results with only four breaths: with the image of red light draw in one breath to fill and cleanse your head and neck, one breath to the torso, one to the lower body and a fourth breath to flood your whole crystal clear body with rainbow light. With further practice, you will be able to master this method with a single breath by simply super-charging your whole mindbody with a rainbow-like relaxation at any time or place that you wish.

8 Symptoms of relaxation

Many of us are more familiar with the symptoms of tension than those of relaxation. Listed below are some frequent indicators of relaxation. Which ones are familiar to you? What others might you add to *your* list?

I know that I'm relaxed when I feel a sense of:

heaviness
lightness
warmth
tingling
yawning
sighing
breathing slower
breathing easier
breathing with belly
openness
connectedness
calm
quiet
peacefulness
flow of feelings
emotional release
body quivers
eyes softening
muscles softening
hands feeling heavier and warmer

Part Two
Concentration

Concentration is like a diamond,
a brilliant focusing of our energy,
intelligence and sensitivity.

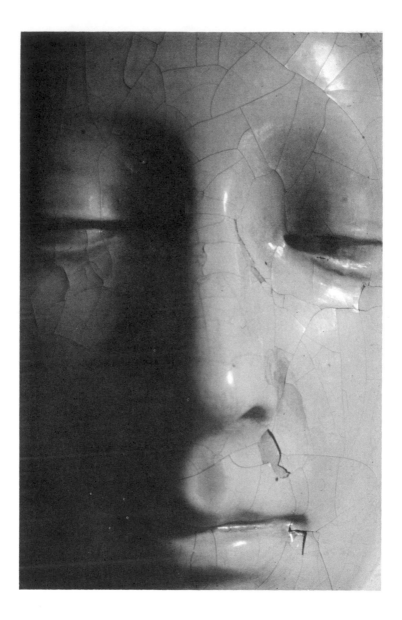

Focusing the mind

Life is learning. The amount of real learning that takes place is directly proportional to our ability to concentrate or focus our attention on any one thing for a period of time. The learning that is meant here is not just the acquisition of knowledge, but the ability to penetrate deeply into the meaning behind superficial knowledge.

By developing our ability to concentrate, we develop our capacity to integrate related thoughts, facts and information into a structural framework that reveals a deeper, more synthesized meaning than that which is immediately apparent to the superficial or unconcentrated observer. The concentrated mind enables us to accelerate our growth and learning because it provides us with direct access to knowing and to understanding the meanings and causes underlying ordinary appearances.

For most people, the distracted and uncontrolled circulation of thoughts and mental impressions or the narrow-minded preoccupation with certain aspects of these impressions is the norm. These distracted and confused states of mind do not lead to peak performance or creative insight. From its usual vantage point of discursive thought or casual observation, our unfocused mind does not have the stability or power to pierce the veil of superficial appearance and to directly perceive the deeper levels of meaning and the underlying interrelationships to which all great scientists and philosophers refer.

The father of modern psychology of consciousness, Dr. William James, was once asked how long it was possible to sustain a focus of concentration upon a single object. After some reflection, he replied that to the best of his knowledge or ability, four seconds was the maximum. For most of us, even that would be a feat! Yet, as we explore the literature on peak performance from the world's great contemplative traditions, we find descriptions of and directions for systematically developing states of concentration and stabilized attention for periods of minutes, hours, even days without distraction.

We have all had a taste of concentration. At different times in our lives, each of us has fully given our attention to a loved one, a beautiful sunset, a resounding symphony or a project that completely absorbed us. And it is possible to train our minds to increase and develop such concentration.

Often cited as the initial indicator that one's practice of concentration is becoming stable is that one's attention can stay unbroken on the count of seven, then twenty-one, then 108 breaths. As this *concentration* grows, even when our attention does wander, the distraction is immediately recognized and we can return our mind to the object of concentration.

In the next phase, concentration matures to become *contemplation*. Here, we begin to experience a sense of connectedness, a flow, between ourself the observer and the object of our attention. Finally, at the third stage of *unification*, we have wholeheartedly and uninterruptedly given our attention to our object. Here, we enter into an intimate relationship with it, knowing it intuitively as though it were one with us. You may have spontaneously experienced this quality of complete concentration some time when you were in love or when your attention was completely captured by something of inspiring beauty.

With practice, our minds will grow more stable, our perception of ourselves and our world will gradually change. New domains of intuitive understanding will be revealed and incorporated into our lives. Our sense of isolation will diminish and we will feel an interrelatedness, an empathy, compassion and respect — for ourselves, each other and the world.

Developing strong concentration is similar to developing physical strength. The patient, persistent practice that the following techniques bring will certainly build your ability to concentrate. Once this skill is developed, a concentrated beam of awareness can be focused upon any activity, leading to a deeper understanding and appreciation of ways to enhance your perception and performance.

As you proceed, remember the following advice:

Be patient with everyone, but above all with yourself. I mean do not be disheartened by your imperfections, but always rise up with fresh courage. How are we to be patient in dealing with our neighbour's faults if we are impatient in dealing with our own. He who is fretted by his own failings will not correct them. All profitable correction comes from a calm and peaceful mind.

St. Francis de Sales

Guidelines for developing concentration skills

Before an instrument can be used it must be created. It is true that most of us learn to concentrate on worldly affairs, but all such effort is directed towards the analysis, synthesis and comparison of facts and ideas, while the Concentration which is a necessary prelude to Meditation aims at unwavering focus on the chosen thing or idea to the exclusion of any other subject. . . complete one pointedness of thought upon the subject in hand, be it a pencil, a virtue, or a diagram imagined in the mind.

Christmas Humphreys

1. *Selecting an object/focus of concentration*

There are literally thousands of objects of attention that have been prescribed for developing concentration. Some ancient traditions would emphasize concentration upon divine attributes such as strength, power, compassion, beauty, mercy, etc. Others recommend contemplation on the gross and subtle elements of earth, water, fire, air and space. Some systems emphasize focusing upon various centres within the body, or upon sacred objects, symbols or prayers.

The simplest and most direct method for developing mental stability and concentration is to focus upon one's own breath. It is easily found, always present, and self renewing — approximately 21,000 times every day. It is certainly the most effective method for people with busy minds and excessive internal dialogue.

Our state of mind and flow of breath are very closely connected. You can observe for yourself the changes in your own rate and flow of breath when you are feeling anxious, angry, joyful, loving, stressed or at peace. Simply by bringing our attention to the respiratory process, the mind moves towards greater calm, clarity and equilibrium.

If you are physically oriented, you might find some simple repetitive movement will help you to develop a continuity of concentration. Some martial art form, a gesture or mudra repeated over and over, a yoga posture or even jogging and cycling can help you begin to develop the initial stages of concentration if you engage in it wholeheartedly.

If you have a devotional orientation, an object of special meaning can serve well in the development of single-pointed concentration. Choose a picture of a source of inspiration or a sacred symbol or object. The repetition of a short prayer or mantra, or the contemplation of some divine aspect may also be a powerful means to wholeheartedly focus your attention.

The breath, however, can be used at the beginning of these sessions to settle you easily into a quiet state of mind. And it would be ideal to end periods of movement, above, with a few moments of watching the breath.

The breath can become a good friend, a reminder to awaken to the nature of our experiences. With the awareness of a single breath we can focus our attention in the moment, release the tensions of our mindbody and move towards greater harmony.

2. *Key to developing concentration*

Once you start to learn to concentrate, you will find that your mind will sway between holding too tightly and too loosely to its object. It is important to find the balance between these two.

So, once you have settled your mind on your object and

you are focusing your attention, relax your mind a little. If you grasp too tightly at your object, your mind will become agitated and the body tense. If you relax too much, however, your attention will wander or fade.

With practice and patience, you will learn to distinguish between these two states of attention and to deepen your concentration.

3. *How long should I practice?*

In the beginning it is recommended to keep your sessions short. Frequent short sessions will in the long run be more beneficial and effective than fewer long ones. If your sessions are too long and you push too hard, you will become tired and frustrated.

Let your practice sessions be like the visit of a dear friend — if they leave before you are tired of them, you look forward to their return. If you approach each session with joy, you will have the enthusiasm to practice focusing your attention, and inevitably it will become stable.

The greater your strength of concentration in your practice sessions, the greater will be your power to focus on what you are doing throughout the day.

> *Wisdom is the harmony between our mind and the laws of reality.*
> *Morality is the harmony between our convictions and our actions.*
> *Concentration is the harmony between our feelings, our knowledge, and our will, the unity of all our creative forces in the experience of a higher reality.*
> Lama Govinda

See *Guidelines for developing relaxation skills* on pp.27—38 for further advice.

1 Self-remembering

If the heart wanders or is distracted, bring it back to the point quite gently...and even if you did nothing during the whole of your hour [of contemplation] but bring your heart back, though it went away every time you brought it back, your hour would be very well employed.
St. Francis de Sales

As you read these words, *know* that you are reading.

Developing our ability to be aware of what we are doing is called self-remembering. This practice enables us to fine-tune our perceptions and actions. It brings calm, clarity and freedom to the mind, qualities that are necessary for recognizing the limiting patterns of habitual thought and actions, and for choosing more creative and effective options. With this awareness we can guide our lives toward attaining the goals we wish to reach.

As I breathe in, I know I am breathing in.
Breathing out, I know I am breathing out.
Listening, I know I am listening.
Touching, I know I am touching.
Lifting, I am aware of lifting.
Sitting down, I am aware of sitting down.
Thinking, I am aware of thinking.
Experiencing fear, I am aware of feeling fear.
Experiencing joy, I am aware of feeling joy.

Intending, I am aware of intending.
Beginning, I am aware of beginning.
Reading, I am aware of reading.
Finishing, I am aware of finishing.

Suggestions:
Simply go for a walk.
Simply listen to music.
Simply eat a meal.

Above all, *keep your mind wholeheartedly on what you are doing*. And when it wanders — as it surely will — simply bring it back to what you are doing, and without self criticism or lecturing yourself, return to your practice of self-remembering.

2 *An antidote to discouragement*

It is easy to feel that your practice session has been a waste of time when much of it is taken up with distraction or agitation. A simple remedy to this, and a way to help develop your concentration is to break up your hour or half-hour or less into many smaller sessions with very short breaks in between. (Also, you could apply this method any time you have a few moments to spare.)

1. Sit comfortably with the spine straight.
2. Gently and completely exhale.
3. As you exhale, softly vocalize the sound Ahhh. Allow the sound to open and flow outwards. Allow your mind to open and flow with the sound as one continuous wave of awareness, until it reaches the moment when distraction or agitation arises.
4. At the first sign of distraction or agitation, immediately stop the session.
5. Relax, take a break for 15–20 seconds. Look around, stretch your legs if you like, then repeat steps 2–5.

Repeat these steps as many times as you like within the time you have allowed for your session. Gradually you will become accustomed to these short spans of continuous attention and applied concentration. Initially your concentration will last for only a few seconds, but with practice you will develop stability, and the depth and duration of your concentration will grow.

As your concentration develops, consciously feel that your mind and the sound of Ahhh are continuously opening outward, even when you stop the Ahhh to take another breath.

3 Zen breathing exercise

*As concentration and attention increase, the mind
becomes clear and balanced. More and more sharply
we see how things are changing in each instant, how
these are ultimately not a source of lasting happiness,
and how the whole mindbody process flows according
to certain laws (karma) empty of any permanent
self... These profound insights become clear simply
from increasing mindfulness, penetrating awareness
of our own process. With these insights wisdom
arises, bringing equanimity, loving kindness and
compassion, for in experiencing the emptiness of self
we see the unity of all beings.*
Jack Kornfield

1. Sit comfortably with your spine straight. Establish a proper motivation for beginning the session.
2. Bring your attention to either the sensation of breath flow at the tip of your nostrils or to your abdomen as you inhale and exhale naturally.
3. Consciously take a few deep breaths, but do not strain. Simply emphasize the movement in order to clarify the sensations that you are attending to.
4. Now, allow the breath flow to find its own natural rhythm. Allow the body to breathe without interference. Allow the inhalations and exhalations to come and go, effortlessly keeping a keen awareness of the process.

5. Gently and unwaveringly allow your attention to float on the changing rhythms of your in and out breath. Whenever your attention wanders or becomes diffused — and it quite often will — gently but firmly bring your awareness back to the breath.

Initially, it may be helpful to count your breaths with each exhalation up to ten. When you reach ten, start your count again. If your attention is distracted, or fades out, begin at one again. The aim is not to arrive anywhere but to develop the capacity to be fully present in each moment, one after another.

Don't be discouraged or disheartened by distractions or mental dullness. This is to be expected. With practice, you will be able to catch the distractions and bring your attention back to the breath. Eventually your concentration will stabilize, and even though distraction will still arise you will be able to stay unwaveringly upon your object of concentration. You will have developed the capacity to bring a continuum of undistracted, deeply penetrating attention to whatever field of perception or contemplation you choose.

The force of the mind and its illuminating, penetrating capacity, once it is developed, is similar to the power and coherence of a laser beam compared to the flickering candle of our ordinary distracted states of consciousness. This power and clarity of the finely-tuned mind is one of the most useful tools that a human being can develop.

4 Breathing easy

Sit comfortably and relax, and bring your awareness to your breathing. As you breathe out, naturally dissolve and let go of all the negative energy that you wish to be free from. As you breathe in, allow the breath to naturally and effortlessly fill you with the positive qualities you want to be energized by. Allow the breath to fill you as a natural reflex to the deep exhalation.

Think of a word that reflects the quality you wish to be filled with — for example, *relaxing, harmonizing, balancing, energizing, peace, patience*. See that particular quality as luminous energy that, as you inhale, rises within you, fills you and flows through you, completely permeating your bodymind. Allow this light energy to dissolve all your negative states of mind, tension or pain. Allow the natural vitality of life to awaken within you.

As you exhale, say to yourself *dissolving, melting, releasing* or *letting go*. Feel the tensions, thoughts, cares and painful states of bodymind flowing out of you and melting away. Emphasize the long, slow exhalation, then allow the inhalation to come naturally, effortlessly.

Place your hands on your belly and quietly breathe in and out of them. Allow your belly to gently rise and fall as the breath flows through you.

After a few minutes, allow the breath, after naturally filling your belly, to rise up to the center of your chest and fill you as though a bubble of breath were filling you from within. Exhale through an imaginary hole in the center of your chest and allow your heart to open...

Breathing into your hands...bringing the air up to fill your heart...opening the heart...exhaling...opening and letting go.

5 Abdominal breathing

When under stress, most of us tend to breathe in short, shallow breaths, primarily by expanding our chests. This thoracic breathing is not the most efficient way to breathe. Not only does it prevent the lungs from filling and emptying completely, it can also contribute to increased muscle tension.

During stressful situations, it is especially important that we breathe from our abdomen, not just our chest. Abdominal breathing relaxes the muscles, massages the internal organs and allows more oxygen to energize our system.

The ideal times to practice abdominal breathing are when you are feeling tense or anxious or in need of energizing your body or calming your mind. Just a few of these complete breaths are wonderfully calming and won't be noticed during a meeting or a phone call. This simple procedure is *very* effective.

1. Sit comfortably with your spine straight.
2. Exhale completely.
3. Inhale very slowly, allowing the breath to enter effortlessly through your nose. At the same time push out your abdomen as though it were a balloon expanding. Move your chest as little as possible.
4. After your abdomen is stretched, expand your chest with air. This fills the middle part of your lungs.
5. Allow your abdomen to pull in slightly and your shoulders and collar bones to rise. This fills the upper part of your lungs.

6. Hold your breath for about five seconds. At this point, every part of your lungs is filled.

7. Slowly begin to exhale through your nose. As you do so, gently allow your abdomen to come in. This will lift your diaphragm and allow your lungs to empty. Proper exhalation releases used air and opens space for fresh air to enter.

(At times you may become slightly dizzy. Once you become more familiar with the technique, however, it can be done easily and comfortably.)

6 Concentration: the simple nine-part breath

As a preliminary to meditation practice, some version or variation of the following concentration technique is recommended.

This involves alternating inhalations and exhalations through the left and right nostrils as indicated below. You can either close the opposite nostril with your thumb and index finger or simply focus on one nostril at a time. Do not force or hold the breath, simply allow it to flow deeply, slowly and at a natural rhythm.

1. Inhale right, exhale left (three times each).
2. Inhale left, exhale right (three times each).
3. Inhale both, exhale both (three times each).

With each inhalation imagine drawing in pure, clear, vital energy in the form of light. Imagine it flowing through you, washing your dense and subtle bodies clean and clear. If you lose track of where you are in the sequence, return to the beginning and start again. Once you become familiar with this basic sequence, even visualizing this breath flow pattern will be sufficient to bring about the harmonizing and balancing result.

If you have difficulty breathing through your nose due to allergies or congestion, visualizing and imagining that your breath is moving through the nostrils in this way will often be an effective means of clearing your sinuses.

In addition to the image of inhaling pure white light or vital energy, the following visualization is also recommended as a means of further balancing and harmonizing the mind-body:

1. As you exhale through the left nostril, imagine breathing out all your attachment and desire towards ideas, objects, perceptions or states of mind. Visualize them as dark-red in colour.

2. As you exhale through your right nostril, imagine breathing out all your anger, resentment and frustration. Visualize them as smoke.

3. As you exhale through both nostrils, imagine breathing out all your confusion, ignorance, pride and any other mental state that obscures your perception and understanding of the true nature of yourself and the world around you. Visualize these as darkness.

Each time you inhale, breathe in light. As you exhale, imagine that all your mental and emotional confusions, your darkness and dullness of mind dissolve completely into space, atomized and utterly gone. This is an excellent technique to apply frequently throughout the day, whenever you need to clear and focus your mind. (See: Balancing breath, brain and mind, pp. 194–196).

7 Contemplative practice

*Our discovery of God is in a way God's discovery of
us. We know Him in so far as we are known by Him,
and our contemplation of Him is a participation in
God's contemplation of Himself. We become
contemplatives when God discovers Himself in us. At
that moment, the point of our contact with God opens
up and we pass through the center of our souls and
enter eternity.*
Thomas Merton

If you have a devotional orientation, the most effective
object for your development of concentration might be a
statue or picture of, say, Jesus, Mary, Buddha, a great saint or
special teacher. Gazing at or visualizing one of these images
or even a sacred symbol, or reciting a prayer or mantra,
could well be effective as a means for collecting your mind
and bringing it to a calm state of concentration.
1. Select an object with special meaning.
2. Wholeheartedly devote your mind and body to this object
   for a chosen period of time.
3. Whenever your mind wanders, gently return it.
4. When you finish, relax, rejoice and give thanks.
5. Carry over this calm and clarity into your next endeavor.
   Allow yourself to go deeply into your contemplation. As
you observe the object of concentration, let your mind settle

upon it, relaxed yet alert. As you breathe in and out, feel a flow of energy and information between you and the essence of your object of contemplation. Let your mind move into it. Let its essential nature permeate you and reveal itself to you. Imagine, sense or feel the essential truth of this image, mantra, sacred symbol or prayer and let it resonate deep within you.

The most beautiful and most profound emotion that we can experience is the sensation of the mystical. It is the sower of all true science. He to whom this emotion is a stranger, who can no longer wonder and stand rapt in awe is as good as dead. To know that what is impenetrable to us really exists, manifesting itself as the highest wisdom and the most radiant beauty which our dull faculties can comprehend only in their most primitive forms — this knowledge, this feeling, is at the center of true religousness. My religion consists of a humble admiration of the illuminable superior who reveals himself in the slightest details we are able to perceive with our frail and feeble minds. That deeply emotional conviction for the presence of a superior reasoning power, which is revealed in the incomprehensible universe, forms my idea of God.
Albert Einstein

8 *Spheres of mind*

Before me peaceful
Behind me peaceful
Under me peaceful
Over me peaceful
Around me peaceful
Navajo

Sit comfortably with your spine straight and your body relaxed. For a few minutes allow your attention to follow the breath or do the nine-part breathing mentioned earlier.

With your eyes closed or slightly open, reach out into the space in front of you and imagine that you are catching hold of a ball in the palm of your hand. Bring this imaginary ball closer to you and add a sense of vividness to its shape and size. Now imagine that in an instant this transforms into a ball of brilliant white light, three-dimensional, transparent, luminous and lacking solidity. Imagine that this ball of light radiates a sense of quiet calm and well-being. As you breathe, feel this ball of light come to rest at the center of your chest. Rest your attention here, effortlessly. Whenever it wanders, return to the inner visualization of a radiant sphere at the center of your chest.

If you feel a tightness in your chest when using the image above, or your mind is too restless to focus, the following variation can be used instead.

Establish the image of a luminous sphere shining at the center of your chest. Now, regardless of what direction you are actually facing, mentally orient yourself as though you were facing east. Imagine that this sphere shoots straight out in front of you, beyond the eastern horizon to a place hundreds, thousands or millions of miles away. Rest your mind on this sphere in the distant space. Experience the freedom of mind to reach out and extend itself farther and farther without any limitation.

If the mind begins to lose interest or drift off to thoughts, once again establish the image of the radiant sphere at your chest. This time shift your attention to the western horizon behind you and vividly imagine sending the sphere out infinitely far in that direction. Rest your mind there. Again, when the mind wanders, reestablish the image at your heart.

With the next cycle, send the mind-sphere off to the southern direction to your right. Imagine the sphere hovering and radiating light thousands and millions of miles to your right. Allow the mind to rest there undistracted and at ease. As before, when your attention wanders or fades, shift again, this time to focus on a sphere of light in space over the northern horizon to your left. With each phase of this practice take as long over the visualization as feels comfortable.

Traditionally, you would now continue with the horizon in front of you to your left and right, and then behind you to your left and right, and even above and far below you. In any case, you should simply let the mind rest on this luminous sphere, this extension of your mind going out into the far distance. Spend as much time as you need to get the feeling of the expansive, limitless nature of your mind.

Finally, expand your mind to encompass all the spheres that you have sent out in all directions along with the original one at your heart. Lucidly and effortlessly rest your mind in this experience of simultaneous expansion to all these directions.

The reason for changing directions in this method is to introduce an element of novelty, freshness and play. Therefore wait until just before you have lost interest in the direction you are focusing on before changing to another. Remember that the purpose of this method is two-fold. Firstly, to stabilize, collect and focus the mind upon what you are doing. Secondly, to introduce you to the open, luminous, unimpeded nature of your mind. If your mind were limited in its scope, how could it reach out to infinity in any direction you choose?

The expansive, luminous, knowing quality of your mind is not limited to the ordinary confines of your body and senses. It is unlimited, omnidirectional and able to reach out into any number of directions in an instant. This method helps you to begin dispelling the misperception of your ordinary limited sense world. Try and do frequent practice with these extraordinary mental muscles at moments throughout the day.

At first the meditator feels like his mind is tumbling
like a river falling through a gorge

in mid-course, it flows slowly like
the gently meandering River Ganges

and finally, the river
becomes one with the great
vast Ocean, where the Lights
of Son (self) and
Mother (ground of being)
merge into one.
Tilopa

9 Concentration with a natural object

In a flash, the violent mind stood still. Within without are both transparent and clear. After the great somersault, the great void is broken through.

Oh, how freely come and go the myriad forms of things!
Han Shan

Many of us have touched a state of deep concentration during our time with nature. Watching the sun rise, a flowing stream, gazing upon a flower, a cloud or rain drops on a still pool, our minds have become clear, quiet and deep. At other times, the chirp of crickets, the sound of breaking waves or a babbling brook have washed away our agitation and left us calm and collected.

1. Select a natural object or process.
2. Attend to it wholeheartedly.
3. Open yourself to let it come in to you, to receive its light, sound, vibration and life into yourself.
4. Open your heart and mind to embrace and be pervaded by it.
5. As you watch, listen or feel it, enter into a deep, quiet communion with this natural phenomena. Allow its essential nature and hidden qualities to reveal themselves intuitively.

The sense of wonder is based on the admission that our intellect is a limited and finite instrument of information and expression, reserved for specific practical uses, but not fit to represent the completeness of our being . . . It is here that we come in direct touch with a reality which may baffle our intellect, but which fills us with that sense of wonder which opens the way to the inner santuary of the mind, to the heart of the great mystery of life and death, and beyond into the plenum void of inner space from which we derive our conception of an outer universe that we mistake for the only genuine reality. In other words, our reality is our own creation, the creation of our senses as well as of our mind, and both depend on the level and the dimensions of our present state of consciousness.

Lama Govinda

10 Concentration while walking

*One may start practice with a pure concentration
exercise and then change to awareness of process.
Initially some teachers prefer using a concentration
technique to enable the meditator to still his
wandering, undisciplined mind. Later they direct this
concentration to the mindbody process to develop
wisdom. Other teachers attempt to start directly
watching the process, by focusing on changing
sensations, feelings or thoughts. This approach must
still concern itself with the development of mental
qualities of tranquility and concentration before any
insight will develop. Buddha taught both approaches
at different times according to the needs of his
students. Much of our time in any day can be spent
walking. This technique can help us use walking as a
means for developing concentration.*
Jack Kornfield

1. Count your first five steps.
2. With the next step, begin at one again and count up to six steps.
3. With the next step, begin at one again and count up to seven steps.
4. Continue counting in this way until you reach ten.
5. Now, begin again, counting your steps from one to five.
6. Repeat the entire sequence up to ten steps as many times as you like.

If you lose track at any point — and you most likely will —
begin again at the cycle of five steps.

Note that if you begin on your right foot, the cycles
ending in five and six steps will end on the right foot. Those
ending at seven and eight will end on the left foot. And
those ending at nine and ten will end on the right foot. This
pattern will reverse with each full cycle.

Remember...
When you walk, walk.
and when you run, run.
By all means, don't wobble!
Zen poem

Part Three
Meditation

*Meditation opens the mind of man to the greatest
mystery that takes place daily and hourly; it widens
the heart so that it may feel the eternity of time and
infinity of space in every throb; it gives us a life
within the world as if we were moving about in
paradise; and all these spiritual deeds take place
without any refuge into a doctrine, but by the simple
and direct holding fast to the truth which dwells in
our innermost beings.*
Suzuki Roshi

What is meditation?

At the heart of each great religious tradition is a wisdom school of transformational teachings. While the exoteric religious teachings provide many guidelines and examples of how best to conduct one's outer life, the more psychological and meditative teachings of the esoteric schools have provided practitioners throughout the ages with practical and systematic guidelines for transforming and fully maturing the mind and emotions.

In Western cultures, most of these lineages of teachings have died out. In many Eastern cultures, these teachings have flourished in an environment that has valued, nurtured and encouraged the investigation and cultivation of the potential for the full development and maturation of the human capacity for power, wisdom and compassionate love.

Today, meditation techniques are undergoing a secular revival as our state oracle of science discovers and proclaims the benefits of meditation as a remedy to the epidemic stress of modern life. In the last ten years, it has become increasingly common to find the practice of meditation encouraged in high level corporate creativity sessions, in locker rooms, during coffee breaks, before and after work, prior to tests, before athletic competition, even in military maneuvers. With the use of relaxation, imagery, attention training or meditation many people are being introduced to powerful and highly effective mental technologies of personal transformation that have been the cherished and often secret practices of many ancient traditions.

This trend has sometimes been attributed as a shift from left to right brain thinking, or as the meeting of Eastern and Western views and values in life. For our purpose here, let's consider meditation as a skillful means for moving from the pain of our personal and planetary fragmentation towards the direct intuitive understanding of our wholeness and potential as human beings.

Meditation techniques are best understood as methods of mental training, and the goal of meditation is two-fold. It involves (1) the *conscious cultivation* of mental qualities that enhance our understanding, power and love, and (2) the *intentional transformation* or lessening of those mind states that block these qualities.

A person well versed in inner science traditions has access to a veritable apothecary of meditative antidotes to disturbing mind states as well as to potent methods for enhancing and developing wholesome and helpful states of mind. Mastering our mind in these ways, we will inevitably develop mastery over our physical and verbal expressions and our relationship with the world.

Choices in a meditator's life are very simple: Do those things that contribute to your awareness, and refrain from those things that do not.
Sujata

A contemporary view of meditation sees it as a way of training or disciplining our *attention*. Most of us have little or no control over the attention we give to any event or experience. It is drawn compulsively towards those sensory and mental experiences that bring us pleasure and away from those that displease or hurt us. And we can't even enjoy the pleasures: how often have you looked forward to a special meal and then been so distracted that you hardly tasted or enjoyed a bit? Or been at a movie or concert and missed whole sections of it because your attention wandered off into fantasies or worries or sleep?

By training your mind in meditation you will learn to be wholeheartedly present in the moment. Distractions will inevitably arise, but with practice we can quickly recognize and reduce them.

There are thousands of meditation techniques from many different traditions, but all could be classified as belonging to either one or a combination of three categories: (1) *concentration*, (2) *receptive* and (3) *reflective*.

By using *concentration meditation* we learn to intensify and stabilize our attention. The aim is to focus single-pointedly and uninterruptedly upon an object or activity.

Traditionally, the practice involves focusing upon one's own breath, a movement form such as a ritual or the martial arts, a mantra or prayer, the visualization of an image or the contemplation of a mental quality. The meditator attends to this concentration in a relaxed yet firm way and whenever the attention wanders it is immediately returned to the object of concentration.

The qualities being developed in this practice are mental stability, lucid awareness and primarily the ability to apply the mind single-pointedly. Your practice of this meditation also helps you to develop introspective alertness, which recognizes and is thus an antidote to distraction, and will-power or determination, which enables you to keep your mind on what you are doing.

Receptive meditation emphasizes the development of a choiceless mindful attention to whatever arises within the sphere of one's experience. Traditionally, the practice of zen, mahamudra, mindfulness, choiceless awareness, self-remembering and prayer of the heart would belong to this category.

Suspended in wonder as we gazed into the depths of the night sky, or listened to the sounds of silence or marvelled at...each of us has known spontaneous, yet fleeting moments of this type of meditative awareness.

Receptive meditation strengthens this sense of wonder and appreciation, enabling you to effortlessly yet precisely attend to the multisensory totality or your experience unfolding moment to moment.

Receptive meditation strengthens your ability to effortlessly and precisely attend to the totality of your experience as phenomena arise and fade away.

The interplay of concentration and receptive meditation allows you to develop the powerful capacity to examine and intuitively understand the deep nature of your experiences. The penetrating insight that you develop can be applied to comprehending the very subtle quantum dynamics of the perceived world and of the nature of your own mind perceiving it. You come to understand the dynamic and pervasive interrelatedness of everything, and you feel intimately and naturally a part of everything around you.

In the practice of *reflective* or *analytical meditation* you engage in reflection, analysis or contemplation of a question, a principle, an idea or an experience. Traditionally one would use this type of meditation to look deeply at the meaning of life, death, relationship and responsibility to the world or to the conscious development of qualities such as confidence, patience, endurance and a centered strength of mind.

In our day to day life and work, reflective meditation provides us with a powerful and effective method for focusing our attention upon personal of professional questions in order to find a creative solution or insight. Reflective meditation is also a powerful tool for understanding and dispelling the obstacles that the meditator may encounter in the practice of concentration or receptive meditation.

Before you start your receptive or reflective meditation, you would find it helpful to first devote a few minutes to stabilizing and energizing your attention with a concentration technique. Once the mind has become stable and lucid, enter into your receptive or reflective meditation.

Guidelines for developing meditation skills

1. Clean and clear space

Create a special space for yourself, either a room or a corner, and use it only for your meditation and heartfelt study or contemplation. Put in this space only those things that help your meditation. Arrange in a pleasing way the pictures and objects that energize the qualities of heart and mind that you are trying to nurture. Arrange a comfortable seat for yourself.

Keep the space clean and clear, as though you were always expecting a special guest. Enter it with respect, and nurture and be energized by the peace, beauty and healing qualities of it.

2. Proper posture

Our posture, physical condition and health directly effect the state of our mind. It is especially important, therefore, to sit comfortably during meditation, with the spine straight and the body relaxed. In the beginning, you may be distracted by tension, pain or restlessness or an inability to find a comfortable position. You may find it helpful to do a few minutes of some simple stretching or yoga excercises before you sit.

You may sit either in a chair or cross-legged. If you would like to learn to sit cross-legged, then start your session with a few minutes of stretching and sit for a while with your legs crossed, increasing the length of time each day as it becomes more comfortable. But remember, don't push too hard.

When sitting cross-legged it is important to have your butt higher than your knees. Experiment with different height cushions until you are comfortable.

Another alternative is to kneel on a small meditation bench or over a large pillow. This posture has the advantage of taking much of the pressure off your knees. You may lie on your back too, but it is not encouraged if you tend to fall asleep.

Whichever way you choose to conduct your meditation session, remember that it is important for your head and spine to be as straight as possible in order for your mind to be alert. With practice, you will learn to bring a meditative mind to standing, lying down and even walking.

3. *Relaxation and alertness*

We are all familiar with the continuum of arousal — from the deep relaxation of sleep to hyperactivity and alertness. Generally, for most of us, our experience of deep relaxation completely lacks alertness and is at best dull and dreamlike. And at the very height of alertness we are the very opposite of relaxed, experiencing physical tension and mental agitation. Both of these extremes are far from the relaxed yet alert, calm delight of meditative equipoise.

During meditation it is necessary to find the dynamic balance between being over alert — that is, distracted — and over relaxed — that is, dull. Especially in the beginning, much of your session might be spent finding this balance, bringing the mind back from distraction or dullness to a state of relaxed alertness. Eventually, you will become familiar with this state of being. During your meditation sessions you will be able to be deeply relaxed as well as extremely lucid, and during your day to day life you will find that your view of the way things are will be less conditioned and obstructed. With this deepening understanding, you will be better able to optimize your response to the challenges and opportunities of each moment with more creative and compassionate attitudes, words and actions.

4. Concentration

Concentration is the foundation of meditation. Whatever the technique, it is necessary to have the ability to place your attention on the object of meditation and hold it there without distraction. With patience and practice, your mind will become calmer, more powerful and able to apply itself to any task with precision and understanding.

As discussed in Part Two, any object or activity can be used for the specific development of concentration. In the following meditations, the same principle would apply: whenever your mind wanders, simply return it to the object of your meditation.

You might find it useful to start your meditation session with a few minutes of one of the concentration techniques, particularly a breathing technique.

5. Thoughts to energize your meditation

Consider the precious opportunity that this human existence gives us. By practicing meditation we can realize and express our enormous potential. This is a great gift.

Then consider impermanence. Whatever is born will die, whatever appears will disappear. The one exception is the open, clear, limitless space of our minds. Recognizing this, we understand that the mind is the most important thing. We also see that we really don't know how much time we have to recognize and train the mind.

Thinking about cause and effect, we understand that we create our own lives. What we experience today is the result of what we did, thought and said earlier, and what we do, think and say now will become our future.

Finally, we consider why we should work with our minds. The long term result, the experience of enlightenment, is more joyful, more intense and complete than anything we have known up until this moment, and once found can never be lost. And secondly, there is so much suffering in the world, and our ability to benefit others is very limited if we are confused ourselves.

So, for ourselves and others, we want to place our trust in those who can help us and in the teachings and methods that help us to master our mind and to become truly wise and kind.

6. *Trust*

For all these reasons, then, we seek a refuge from the chaos and confusion within and around us. Like a child taking refuge in its mother, or hikers seeking shelter from a storm, we seek a refuge of sanity in a crazy world.

Outwardly, we place our trust in the teachers who remind us through their example, their kindness and their teachings that it is possible to become free from our mental and emotional confusions and to become wise and kind as well. We find strength and guidance in the teachings that show us how to master our minds and find freedom and understanding in our lives. Likewise, we find a refuge in the community of friends and companions who share our study, practice and investigation of how meditation is practically applied to meeting the challenges and opportunities of daily life.

Inwardly, the teacher reflects the seed of our own potential for deep understanding and genuine kindness. Oral and written teachings point our minds towards the unspeakable wisdom that shines like the sun and moves within our hearts, the real mystery that precedes life and endures beyond death. Our companions along the way remind us of the community of people who, from the beginning of time, strove to find the same understanding and who preserved and passed the teachings on.

Meditation does not happen in a vacuum, devoid of relationship and sharing with others, whether you are sitting alone in a cave or an office, or meditating in a group. Affirming and trusting your relationships with others and your connectedness with the universe will offer you protection and peace of mind, and will inspire your meditation practice.

7. *Proper motivation*

As you begin each session, remind yourself of why you are sitting down to meditate. Why are you giving yourself this gift of time for centering, harmonizing and fine-tuning? To avoid pain? To be happy? To find peace? To rest or energize?

Remember, as you grow in clarity and peace of mind you directly contribute to bringing peace and understanding to others. And remember, as you develop patience towards the people and situations that previously triggered frustration, you will be filling the universe with compassion instead of anger, understanding instead of confusion.

Our intentions reflect back to us an echo of the same energy. How often have you seen actions motivated by fear emphasize the paranoia of a situation? And how often has your love and care touched and opened the heart of another?

Remember, it is not what you do but how and why you do it that really matters. You always have a choice, so use it wisely and creatively.

8. *Monitor your meditation*

Your meditation session is likely to go through several phases. Once you have settled down you should stabilize your attention by doing a few moments of a concentration technique. Then you can apply your mind to whatever meditation, either reflective or receptive, that you have chosen. Throughout the session, you should use your *introspective alertness* to monitor the quality of the focus of your attention. In this way you can recognize when your attention has wandered off or faded away. If you find it difficult to stay with the meditation because of too much distraction or dullness, you will find it useful to again do a few minutes of a concentration technique, especially watching the breath. Then, once again you can return to your main meditation.

9. *Dedication and sharing*

Take a few moments at the end of each session to consciously extend the positive energies that you have accumulated.
Radiate out into space warmth, light and love and imagine it
touching others as a vibration that calms, energizes, heals,
comforts and nourishes. Be creative! Imagine you are
playing a mental video game. Beam all your positive feelings
to your friends, family, people you feel neutral towards,
even your enemies. Realize that they all, just like you, want
to be happy, want to escape suffering and pain, and desire
to make the most of their lives. Thus, in your own way, you
can make the world a more peaceful place to be in.

In this way, you can see that the time you take to master
stress is not selfish. In fact, it is an active form of accepting
responsibility for and contributing meaningfully to the lives
of others. Though at first, these mental training techniques
may seem imaginary or conceptual, with practice you will
find that you *are* helping − yourself and others.

10. *Carry-over practice*

Through your practice of meditation, it is possible to develop many of your previously latent positive qualities.
Having used the short time of your quiet meditation to
touch and develop the peace, clarity, understanding, kindness and vitality that is a part of you, you now face the challenge of carrying these qualities into dynamic action as you
move through the world. Throughout the day, consciously
recall and re-energize these feelings. Particularly when you
start to rush and tumble, internally pause and move toward
the sense of harmony that you experienced earlier in your
meditation. Periods of quiet, undistracted meditation are
precious opportunities to get in touch with qualities that
will gradually grow and pervade even your busiest activities.

You will find that *any* activity can become an opportunity to train your mind, develop concentration, refine your awareness or practice kindness. Live in a creative and meditative way, as though your life were a dream and you are busy waking up.

11. *Choosing a practice*

Your practice of the relaxation and concentration techniques in the previous chapters will greatly aid your meditation. Begin each session with a few minutes of a relaxation or breathing exercise to calm your bodymind – an essential ingredient for successful meditation.

As you become more familiar with meditation, choose the techniques that best suit your temperament and natural inclinations. Remember that each technique is an antidote to a particular difficulty and a means of strengthening certain qualities of mind. If, for example, you have difficulty with anger, then you should meditate on forgiveness (page 148), loving kindness (page 154) and the meditations on pages 151–166. If you are experiencing physical discomfort or disease, the hollow body meditation (page 133), giving and taking meditation (page 161) and pain techniques (page 190) may be useful. If your mind tends to be tight and narrowly focused, the listening meditation (page 103), continuum (page 105), thoughts (page 111), hollow body (page 133) and matrix of mind (page 179) will be helpful to open and relax your mind.

If you are particularly interested in understanding your mind, the meditations on pages 107–114 will be helpful. If you are devotionally inclined, then the meditation on the teacher (page 163), contemplative practice (page 77) and a devotional approach to all the other meditations will be fruitful.

Trust your heart and your intuitive sense of what you need, but also, understand the importance of being guided by an experienced teacher.

12. *Finding a teacher*

The most effective way to learn anything is to study with someone who has already mastered it. Meditation is certainly no exception. Our mind can be compared to a remarkable musical instrument that is capable of generating the sweetest of music, yet often plagued with chaotic and noisy sounds. If we sincerely wish to learn to play beautiful music, we must study with a master who knows the instrument inside and out. In order to develop a clear, calm, joyful and loving mind, we need the guidance of someone who thoroughly understands how the mind works and how it can be transformed.

How do you find a qualified teacher? It is not always so easy. The qualities to look for in a teacher include compassion, knowledge and insight, morality, sincerity and skill, both in teaching and in the way they live their life. From your own side, you should have confidence in your teacher and be able to communicate well with him or her. However, don't set out on a frantic guru hunt! Take it easy. It may be a matter of years before you meet the person who can answer your questions and be this special friend and teacher.

Meanwhile, you can practice meditations such as those described here and seek the advice of any meditators whose qualities you admire. Learn to trust your *own* intuitive wisdom, your *own* inner guru, to tell you whether you are heading toward or away from your goal.

> *Sitting quietly, doing nothing*
> *Spring comes and the grass grows by itself.*

See *Guidelines for developing relaxation skills* on pp. 27–38 for further advice.

Meditation techniques are discovered naturally by infants and little children: holding their breath, staring unblinking, standing on their heads, imitating animals, turning in circles, sitting unmoving and repeating phrases over and over until all else ceases to exist. Stop thinking that meditation is anything special. Stop thinking all together! Look at the world around you as if you had just arrived on Planet Earth. Observe the rocks in their natural formations, the trees rooted in the ground, their branches reaching to the sky, the plants, animals and the interrelationships of each to the other. See yourself through the eyes of a dog in a park. See a flower through its essence. See a mountain through its massiveness. When the mind allows its objects to remain unmolested, there may be no mind and no object — just breathless unity.

Surya Singer

1 *Doing what we love to do*

*The first step in growth is to do what we love to do
and to become aware of doing it.*
Sujata

What do you really enjoy doing? Have you ever considered that this could be an excellent meditation for you?

Doing what we love to do with awareness *is* meditation. Meditation is not the activity, but the quality of attention that we bring to the activity. Any activity of our daily life, approached with the intention of developing concentration and clarity, can become a meditation.

1. Choose an activity you enjoy.
2. Determine that you will bring your full attention to it.
3. Slowly, carefully and mindfully begin. Remain relaxed, giving your wholehearted attention to what you are doing.
4. Whenever your attention wanders or fades, gently return to being fully aware of what you are doing. If tensions arise, relax and smile playfully to yourself.
5. When the activity or time period that you had designated is over, pause for a few moments to reflect upon the new richness you have discovered in this familiar activity.

In fact, everything that we do throughout the day, even the tasks that we do not like, can become a tool for developing our minds and deepening our concentration.

2 Listening

> At the heart of each of us, whatever our
> imperfections, there exists a silent pulse of perfect
> rythm — a complex of wave forms and resonances
> which is absolutely individual and unique and yet
> which connects us to everything in the universe.
>
> George Leonard

LISTEN...
We are continually hearing information
from the world around and within us.
Minimize distortion by turning down the
volume of your internal dialogue.
Imagine that the universe is about
to whisper the answer to your deepest
questions...and you don't want to miss
it!
LISTEN...
Simply, and without analysis or commentary to
whatever sounds enter the sphere of your
awareness. Don't label the sounds. If you
start thinking, remind yourself to just...
LISTEN...
Effortlessly to sounds.
Let them come to you.
No need to tense or strain.
Trust. Let go of control. Be at ease.
Still...quiet...receptive...and alert...

LISTEN...

    Notice how sounds arise...and fade away...

      Melting into silence or into other sounds.

        Don't try to hold them, allow them to flow...

LISTEN...

    Where do the sounds go?

LISTEN...

    Where do the sounds come from?

LISTEN...

    Experience how the space of your awareness

      effortlessly accommodates an interpenetrating

        symphony of sounds, thoughts, sensations, feelings

        and visions simultaneously. Allow, your

          bodymind to relax into unencumbered clarity...

LISTEN...

    Allow the answers to these questions to

    come as understanding, not as thoughts.

LISTEN...

    And reflect...

    WHO IS LISTENING?...

3 Continuum

There are no ends in life, only processes. Change.
Spiritual reality is physical reality, clearly seen.
Bill Voyd

As you breathe, draw your awareness into this moment.

Exhaling, allow your awareness to flow effortlessly into the next moment. Inhaling, stabilize and focus your awareness into this moment. Exhaling, feel the flow of your being unfolding, moving and continuously expressing itself through the medium of time and space.

Standing in the present, step into the future and leave the past irretrievably behind you. As you move, feel yourself emanating and moving forward through space and time.

Imagine that as you move you trace a pathway of light and energy through the fabric of space and time. Imagine that if you turned around you could actually see this luminous path, like a firefly in the night.

Now, imagine the path you have traced through the world today, during the past week, the last month. Sense the patterns, cycles and rhythms of your goings and comings.

Imagine arising and retracing your steps as you moved around the house, drove to work or school, dropped into your favorite stores, visited friends, went for walks or bike rides. See your life as a continuum of light energy patterns unfolding through space and time.

Imagine the pattern of your continuum unfolding since you were born. Even try and imagine the energy patterns of the body you were in before this one, and the one before that, and so on, back and back. Really feel yourself as a dynamic process expressing and unfolding itself through space and time.

Imagine the tons of universe that have sustained you and that you have burned as air and water and food during your life's — your lives' — journey.

Imagine your moments of being in love, your experiences of joy, of anger. Feel how your energy pervades space and affects the people all around you.

See how a simple apple is a continuum, a fusion of sunlight, water, earth, air, and the trees and apples that came before it. Imagine the kindness and work of the many people and creatures who have caused you to finally have this apple. Where does this apple-energy begin or end? Where does *your* field of energy begin or end?

Imagine your friends and companions. See them as merely a perceptual snapshot of a continuum of being. See the forest, flowers, objects as simply a process. Trace your tie pin, the polyester in your blouse, back to their organic roots in the earth. See everything as interwoven pathways of light and energy unfolding through space and time. People, planets, galaxies, atomic clouds of energy, whirling, unfolding beginninglessly and endlessly through time and space. Thoughts, dreams, fantasies and memories — all the play and process of your mind.

Exhaling, imagine releasing some old grudge or limitation. Inhaling, receive new strength, wisdom and energy. Use your cycles of breath to let go of old limiting postures, attitudes and emotions that keep you from moving freely through life. With each breath, receive inspiration to nurture those qualities you wish to strengthen.

Life is made of moments. What ripens in any moment are seeds sown in the past. In this moment we can consciously sow seeds for happiness and health in the future.

Breathe your awareness into this moment.

As you exhale, allow your continuum to unfold with peace, balance and joy.

4 Investigating the mind

*One should realize that one does not meditate in order
to go deeply into oneself and withdraw from the
world. . . There should be no feeling of striving to
reach some exalted or higher state, since this simply
produces something conditioned and artificial that
will act as an obstuction to the free flow of the
mind. . . When performing the meditation practice,
one should develop the feeling of opening oneself out
completely to the whole universe with absolute
simplicity and nakedness of mind. . . Meditation is not
to develop trance-like states; rather it is to sharpen
perceptions, to see things as they are. Meditation at
this level is relating with the conflicts of our life
situations, like using a stone to sharpen a knife, the
situation being the stone.*
Trungpa Rinpoche

The mind is a process, a continual flow of our intellectual,
emotional and sensory experiences. Usually it wanders
randomly of its own accord along conditioned lines of association and habit. As you learn to watch and understand
this process, your natural yet undeveloped capacity for calm
and clarity grows stronger. Gradually you will notice that
you can take more effective control of your own life and be
less under the influence of compulsive patterns of thought
and emotion.

The following sequence of exercises is excellent for developing insight into how your mind works. For best results,

practice the first exercise for a few days or weeks, or until you have gained some insight, then move onto the next, until eventually you have completed the sequence.

Exercise 1   *Focusing and quieting the mind*

Sit comfortably and take a few minutes to relax. Rest your hands in your lap and quietly and gently smile to yourself. Bring your attention to your breath and feel the sensation of the air flow out of your nostrils. Now, start to count each exhalation, from one to ten. If you lose count, return to one. If you are able to reach ten, start again at one.

You can use this technique at any time during the day, even for a few minutes. The aim is to bring your attention to a keen yet relaxed focus on what you are doing. Don't try too hard to concentrate, but allow your mind to be alert and relaxed. Inevitably your mind will wander, but whenever it does simply return to the next breath. With practice you will gradually find it easier to keep your mind on whatever you are doing.

Exercise 2   *Watching the mind*

Again, sit comfortably, smile to yourself, and watch your flow of breath for a few moments. Allow the turbulence of your wandering mind to subside naturally, and allow the natural clarity and calm of your mind to become apparent.

Rest your hands palm down on your legs and bring your attention to your breath. Whenever your mind wanders off to memories or thoughts of the past, gently tap your left leg. If you notice that your mind wanders off into projected fantasies of future events, gently tap your right leg. With the mind calm yet alert, watch the breath flow, simply noting the excursion of your mind into memories and future fantasies. As the thoughts arise, mentally note 'memory' or 'fantasy,' then return your attention to the breath.

The goal of this exercise is to simply notice the *process* of our thinking minds, without becoming involved in or identifying with the specific *content* of the thoughts themselves.

Exercise 3   Sensory experience

Begin as in the previous exercises, using the breath to help you stabilize and focus your mind. Now, expand your ability to notice your mental process by including sensory experiences. Whenever you become aware of physical sensation either make the mental note 'feeling' or, if you want to be more specific, 'pleasure,' 'pain,' 'tingling,' 'itching,' etc. Do not engage in internal dialogue, but simply and crisply note what you are experiencing and bring your awareness back to your breath. Likewise, when you become aware of other sensors experiences, note 'hearing,' 'tasting,' 'smelling,' 'touching.'

Exercise 4   Emotional feelings

Begin by relaxing your body and focusing your mind with a few moments of watching the breath flow. Then, in addition to noting sensory experiences, also note your emotional experiences. Whenever a particular feeling predominates, note its nature, such as 'anger,' 'sadness,' 'fear,' 'resentment,' 'guilt,' 'anxiety,' or whatever brief mental label that fits. Pay particular attention to experiences of 'liking' and 'disliking.' Once again, do not become involved with the content of the emotions, simply note them and return to awareness of the breath.

Exercise 5   Intending

Once we have become familiar with recognizing our thoughts and feelings as they arise, we will be able to see that prior to every voluntary action there is a mental intention. Begin now to notice this intending phase of your experience.

Mentally note the intention to stand up before getting off a chair; the intention to reach out before you open a door. Note the intention to move, to stop, to speak, to turn, to speed up or slow down, to be harsh or to be kind.

By developing mindfulness of your intention, you will develop greater power for creative choice, for seeing a whole new range of options that we hadn't seen before and that *are* available to us in spite of the habitual and highly conditioned mode that most of us live in. So, as you develop insight into the often unconscious and habitual impulses that direct your behaviour, you will discover even greater freedom and power to choose both what you do and how you do it.

It is inevitable that in the fast pace of daily life you will get caught up and carried along by habitual and conditioned thoughts and emotional feelings, and that you will lose your focus of attention and the ability to consciously choose what to do or say. When you become aware of this, mentally stop, smile to yourself and perhaps even chide yourself playfully — and then *breathe* and allow your thoughts and feelings to move and flow and your sense of strength, calm and clarity to grow.

This is the meaning . . . of increasing or raising consciousness . . . taking functions that ran on automatic that were often incongruent within yourself as well as to an outside observer, and making them more conscious, more congruent, making you less the victim of automatization and more a person who understands his or her own psychological machinery and consciously controls it.

Charles Tart

5 Thoughts

In the development of wisdom, one quality of mind above all others is the key to practice. This quality is mindfulness, attention or self-recollection. The most direct way to understand our life situation, who we are and how our mind and body operate, is to observe with a mind that simply notices all events equally. This attitude of non-judgemental, direct observation allows all events to occur in a natural way. By keeping the attention in the present moment, we can see more and more clearly the true characteristics of our mind and body process.

Jack Kornfield

There are many objects of meditation. While some traditions may focus attention upon a physiological process such as breath or posture, other techniques emphasize attention to the changing nature of thoughts, feelings, sensations, emotions and states of consciousness.

This is a meditation using thoughts. Though many people experience thoughts as a distraction to their meditation practice, thoughts can make an interesting and effective object of meditation. By making thoughts the object of our attention we come to the profound understanding that one is not one's thoughts. We realize that thoughts are merely bubbles floating in the vast ocean of one's mind, or simply clouds that arise, change and pass in the sky of mind. By learning to consciously disidentify from the contents of one's thoughts, one learns to view thinking as a process that will arise and unfold without the need of a 'thinker.' Looking deeply into our thoughts of who we are, we find that we are far more and greater than all the voices and ideas that arise and pass in the open clear space of mind.

Begin by sitting quietly and attending to the natural inflow and outflow of the breath. As thoughts arise within, make a mental note of 'thinking...thinking.' Once recognized, many 'trains of thought' will be derailed and the mind will once again become quiet. Practice noticing the thoughts quickly, before they have swept you off into association and elaboration. As the thoughts subside, simply return to attending to the flow of the breath. Allow thoughts to be like waves on the surface of a vast ocean, or like clouds floating in an incomprehensibly vast sky of mind.

Labelling thoughts

For some people labelling the different kinds of thought processes is helpful. This can be done as follows: When memories arise in the mind, note 'remembering.' When fantasies of the future arise, note 'imagining' or 'planning.' Such labelling can help to strengthen the focus and clarity of the mind and help you to identify and dissect the predominant patterns of thought that you have compulsively identified with and been impelled by throughout your life. In learning to simply recognize thinking as thinking, planning as planning, blaming as blaming, remembering as remembering, we can begin to find our power in the present moment and free ourselves from the prison of misidentifying with the limiting patterns of our thoughts. In this way the power of our minds can be understood and properly directed towards energizing the development of the deeper qualities of humanbeingness.

As you practice this meditation, guard against identifying with the content of the thoughts in the mind. Simply pay close attention to the *process* of thinking rather than the *content* of the thoughts. Pay particular attention to the compulsive and reflexive tendency to generate thoughts about your thoughts and engage in inner commentary about the thoughts. Don't regard thoughts as good or bad, right or wrong, or as hindrances to your meditation practice. As Suzuki Roshi, a great contemporary Zen master, once wrote in his book *Zen Mind Beginners Mind*:

> *When you are practicing Zazen meditation, do not try to stop your thinking. Let it stop by itself. If something comes into your mind, let it come in and let it go out. It will not stay long. When you try to stop your thinking, it means you are bothered by it. Do not be bothered by anything. It appears that the something comes from outside your mind, but actually it is only the waves of your mind and if you are not bothered by the waves, gradually they will become calmer and calmer. . . Many sensations come, many thoughts and images arise but they are just waves from your own mind. Nothing comes from outside your mind. . . If you leave your mind as it is, it will become calm. This mind is called Big Mind.*

Noting and noticing changing states of mind

As the mind becomes more stable and balanced, you may feel that the practice of labelling or noting thoughts, emotions or phases of the breath seems cumbersome. Once you have reached this level of mental subtlety, begin to simply *notice* the inhalation or exhalation, or the type of thought or emotional state without generating a mental label. The practice of mindfully noticing the myriad of arising and passing thoughts, physical sensations, emotional feelings and states of consciousness allows the mind to penetrate more deeply into the essential nature of these experiences.

If you find that the clarity or precision of your attention begins to fade, simply return to breath awareness or mental noting techniques in order to sharpen the focus of your attention. Once the clarity and lucidity of mind has been re-established, let go of 'noting' and return to simply 'noticing' the ever changing flow of states of mind and body which are woven into the fabric of your experience.

We asked the teacher, 'What is the nature of the mind?' He replied with the following meditation:
'At your heart, imagine your mind as a drop of light which is the color of the sky and the size of a mustard seed. Imagine that this luminous drop of mind expands as far as it can. Find which is larger, the expanded drop or the sky.'
For fifteen minutes we sat engaged in this meditation, at which time he said,
'This is the nature and expanse of the mind!'

6 *Kitchen yogi meditation*

The technique that follows was inspired by the insight that all of life's daily activities can be transformed into meditations, even the most mundane and ordinary activities such as washing and chopping vegetables. The key to this transformation lies in the art of paying close *attention* to whatever is happening in the present moment. It is not the activity which determines the quality of mental aliveness but rather the energy of *mindfulness* that we bring to it. We all spend much of our lives doing routine and mechanical chores. Experiment with these guidelines to see how you can transform whatever you are doing into an experience of wakefulness.

1. Begin by grounding yourself. Feel the contact between the two soles of your feet and the floor. Note the feeling of your feet touching the ground and sense that the floor beneath connects to the earth.
2. Knees slightly bent, feel your legs growing down into the earth. Hips, thighs, legs growing down into the earth.
3. Move your awareness next into your navel center, your center of power.
4. Now allow the upper part of your body to open and become alive. As you exhale allow your shoulders to drop. With each exhalation let your eyes be soft and your jaw be loose and soft.
5. With each exhalation come back to your body. Sense your body posture.

6. Be receptive. Allow the visual sensation of the vegetables to come to you as you chop with the knife.
7. There is nothing to do but *feel* the sensation of the knife
   in your hand. Feel its hardness. Become aware of the
   sensation of contact, the touch of your hand on the knife.
   Are you squeezing more than you need to as you chop?
   Soften your grip.
8. Allow the feeling of the vegetable you are holding to
   come to you. Note the quality of its sensations.
9. Feet touching the floor.
10. Knees slightly bent.
11. Moving from the center.
12. Be aware of the breath.
13. Eyes soft.
14. Receive. . . .
15. Stay in touch with sensations.
16. Attend to every moment as if it were your last.
17. Soft and alert. Relaxed and precise.
18. Mindfulness moving from moment to moment.

7 Eating mindfully

Practicing mindfulness of eating can be very revealing. There are many processes going on in the mind and body while we eat. As we bring our attention to the sequence of these processes, deep self-understanding can arise.

For example, the first step in eating is *seeing* the food. Become aware of 'seeing.' The next step is *intending* to reach for it. Become aware of 'intending.' The intention drives the body into action to *reaching* for a bite of the food. Again become aware of the process of 'reaching or moving.' When your hand or fork touches the food there is the sensation of *touching*. Be aware of this experience of *touching*. Next, your arm is raised, *lifting* the food to your mouth.

Carefully notice each phase of the process. As the food comes toward your mouth notice *opening* the mouth, *putting* the food in, *lowering* the arm, *feeling* the texture of the food in the mouth, then *chewing* and *tasting*. Be particularly mindful of the experience of tasting. Notice how, as you chew, the taste disappears. Then *swallowing*. Next, watch how desire for more arises, leading to the intention to reach for another bite.

Experience how one phase seems to mechanically lead to the next as though there is really no one eating, but only a sequence of related events unfolding: intention, movement, touch sensations, tastes, etc. Mindful eating can reveal how what we are is just a sequence of happenings, a process and flow of life energy. It can also mirror to us many of our compulsive attitudes toward consuming the universe or receiving nourishment through all of our senses. As we learn to step back and notice the process as well as the content of our activities, we can begin to recognize and transform many old limiting patterns and choose new and more creative options for how to live our lives.

8 *Walking meditation*

*Every path, every street in the world is your
walking meditation path.*
Thich Nhat Hanh

Notice the sequence of movements as you walk. Standing,
lifting, moving, and placing one foot and shifting your
weight. Then lifting, moving, placing and shifting your
weight to the other foot. Begin by moving slowly. Move no
faster than you are able to move with complete awareness.
This is not a moving meditation so much as an exercise in
developing a continuity of mindful awareness. At times
experiment with walking more swiftly, simply noting each
time a foot touches the ground. Be loose and natural. Experience the flow of movement, moment to moment, with
awareness.

9 *Sleeping meditation*

There are numerous approaches to sleeping meditatively. One method is to simply meditate and relax before you go to bed. You might take a few minutes to center and calm your mind. Then review the day. Appreciate your day and as you notice moments about which you might feel some regret, appreciate the positive lessons that these mistakes may hold for your actions in the days to come. In your heart say 'thank you' to everyone who contributed to your learning and growth today. In your heart give and ask forgiveness where needed and feel as though you can sleep in peace.

One technique for sleeping is to imagine that your bed is within a large luminous lotus bud or a small temple or pavilion of light. Imagine that this space resonates with a healing and regenerating light that infuses you as you sleep. Imagine that the resonance and light of this space surrounds you with a buffer zone against any harsh interferences of the outer world. Imagine that it draws into itself all of the positive energy of the universe that may be helpful for you. Rest deeply, and upon awakening simply dissolve this visualization into rainbow light and absorb its essence into you.

Another method is to imagine that as you sleep you rest your head in the lap of a special teacher or protector who watches over you. Let all of your thoughts and cares be dissolved by their presence. Receive their love, strength and inspiration as you sleep. Upon awakening, dissolve them into rainbow light and melt them into space. This technique can be combined with the previous method.

Yet another technique is, as you lie in bed, imagine that with each breath you become filled with more and more light and space. As you exhale, you and everything in the universe melt into an ocean of light and space. Let your mind completely open like a drop falling into a luminous ocean. Rest deeply and powerfully. Upon awakening, let body and world appear fresh and new.

Once upon a time,
I, Chuang Tzu,
dreamt I was a butterfly,
fluttering hither and thither,
to all intents and purposes a butterfly.
I was conscious only of following my fancies as a
butterfly,
and was unconscious
of my individuality as a man.
Suddenly
I awakened,
and there I lay,
myself again.
Now
I do not know
whether I was then a man
dreaming I was a butterfly,
or whether I am now
a butterfly dreaming
I am a man.
Chuang Tzu

10 *Waking up*

Our truest life is when
we are in our dreams awake
Thoreau

How do we know what reality is? When we dream
at night, we believe it is reality, we feel it, we
experience it. Then we wake up and discard these
beliefs. How do we distinguish the real from the
unreal? Where is last night's dream now? Where is
yesterday's experience?
You may look upon this waking state as a dream. If
you see nighttime dreams and daytime illusions as the
same, this can alleviate suffering. Once you establish
that your experience is a dream, it may not seem so
bad. Dreams are unreal, false ideas, illusions. You can
see that your experience is not as serious as you
thought. Your personality changes and your
relationship with other people and the world is
improved. There are different ways to achieve
realization, but looking upon existence as a dream is
one of the best, because it is very enjoyable, very
satisfying and interesting. For a long time we have
viewed the world in one way — as real, solid, and
concrete. Seeing it differently is very enjoyable.
Everything becomes easier. Nothing is wrong: boredom

*is forgotten. We understand what unity is, what
infinity is — infinite time, infinite space, infinite
consciousness. When you strip away all the layers of
ideas, tensions and frustrations, and uncover the naked
reality of consciousness — where there are no things
to hold onto — there can be nothing wrong. This is not
a fantasy or an escape. This is true. If you can realize
this awareness, the world will reveal itself as a source
of unending delight.*

Tarthang Tulku

11 Reflective meditation

Sit comfortably.
With three deep, full inhalations and exhalations
  relax the body
  quiet and focus the mind.
Quietly observe the flow of breath for a few minutes,
inhaling and exhaling
    with a relaxed, yet alert, quality of attention.
      When your mind wanders, return attention to the
      breath flow.

Next, consider and reflect upon a question, idea, situation,
  experience or anticipated scenario.
    Allow your attention to go deeply into consideration of
    this mental image or idea.
      Investigate and explore the meaning, relationships,
      importance and applications to your life.
Whenever the image or flow of ideas fades out
  Simply return to watching the breath flow.
    When the mind is focused and stable again
      Consider the same or a different idea or situation
      and repeat the investigation described above.

At the conclusion of the session
  take three deep, slow breaths,
    open your eyes, stretch your body
      and most importantly
        apply your insights to your daily life!

When meditation is changed from the breath to
awareness of change, the teacher instructs the
meditator with a specific formula for beginning the
practice of sweeping the attention through the body,
part by part, feeling the impermanence of all touch
and sensation. As the awareness of impermanence
continues, the meditator will see how the power of his
concentration and mindfulness can unblock the flow
of energy in the body, the sweeping becomes more
rapid and more clear. As the body becomes clear for
the flow of energy and the impermanence and change
of all sensations becomes more apparent, the focus of
attention of the meditator moves to the region of the
heart. Now mindfulness and concentration on the
changing sensations and feeling are so strong that all
sensations, even the movement of mind, are
experienced as changing, as vibrations. Perception of
the whole world, matter and mind, becomes reduced
to various levels of vibration in a constant state of
change. The meditator continues to apply his
understanding and growing skill and applies his
penetrating insight to directly experiencing the true
nature of existence.
U Ba Kin

12 A meditation for peace and action

Whether you believe you can or you believe that you can't, you are right.

Henry Ford

As you begin this reflective meditation, mentally project yourself to a time five years into the future. Imagine yourself as you would most like to be, having accomplished the things you'd like to accomplish, learned what you would like to learn and made the contributions you would like to have made.

Now consider:

What are the qualities you have developed in yourself?

What are the most important lessons you have learned?

What contributions do you feel most happy about having made?

In order to make these contributions, how did you have to stop under-estimating yourself?

In order to make these contributions, how did you have to stop under-estimating other people?

In order to make these contributions, what would you have to stop pretending you cannot do?

In order to make these contributions, what strengths would you have to be willing to acknowledge in yourself?

In order to make these contributions, what strengths would you have to be willing to acknowledge in others?

In order to make these contributions, what strengths would you have to be willing to acknowledge in others?

Now, consider what you can do *right now* in order to begin making these contributions.

If it feels right, make a commitment to yourself to make this meditated vision of potential a reality.

13 *Two domains of reality*

*We are luminous beings. We are perceivers. We are
an awareness. We are not objects. We have no
solidity. We are boundless. The world of objects and
solidity is a way of making our passage on earth
convenient. It is only a description that was created to
help us. We or rather our reasons forget that the
description is only a description and thus we entrap
the totality of ourselves in a vicious circle from which
we rarely emerge in our lifetime. . . We are perceivers.
The world that we perceive is an illusion. It was
created by a description that was told to us since the
moment we were born.*
Don Juan

We live in a world with two domains of reality. There is the
domain of conventional reality in which I am me and you
are you, where this is a book, where objects have names and
defined relationships. Then there is the domain of ultimate
reality, the quantum soup, the field of undifferentiated
morphic resonance, the domain of spacetime and energy
that is completely empty of isolated entities and which is the
wholeness of all fields and continuums of interrelated energy
and life.

Bringing an awareness of these two realities into our daily
life can help us in so many ways. Certainly, we will develop
more respect, a more sacred attitude, towards the people
and things that surround us.

Bring your mind to the following considerations throughout the day.

An old Zen approach is to ask 'What is this?' When confronted with an object, a situation, don't attempt to analyze it, simply enquire, 'What is this,' and let the mind gain direct insight into it by being completely open, receptive, alert and investigative.

Another approach is to say to ourselves, 'I'm only labelling this as . . . .'
Your labelling or naming is simply an imputation of a concept upon a field of phenomena. Understand the relativity of your imputations and mental projections. Open your mind to glimpse the nature of things unnamed and before thought, fresh, alive and uncontrived.

In considering yourself, investigate and reflect, 'Who am I?'
Listen for the answers that arise as the changing flow of physical sensations, emotional feelings, states of mind or consciousness. Beware of any idea that you impute upon the totality of the process that is you. Experience and realize that you are far more than your thoughts of who you are.
Who are you really?

14 *Meditation on the four elements*

Begin this meditation with a few minutes of relaxation and breath awareness. Now bring your attention to the earth element of your body — that aspect of your existence which is dense and solid. Feel the massiveness of your body, its weight and form. As you breathe, contemplate and feel the element of earth experienced as form, density, mass and weight.

Now shift your focus of attention to the water element — that aspect of your embodiment and of your world which is fluid and cohesive. Feel or imagine this dynamic fluidity as blood, lymph and other waters of life flowing within your body. Sense and imagine this water element flowing through the world in which you live.

The element of fire is associated with the warmth, light and heat of your body, and of the world. Feel this inner heat, this vital warmth that dissipates at death. Experience how this element of heat and light is evident as it radiates in all living beings and through the world around you.

The air element is related to the spaces of the internal cavities, movement and the flow of the breath. This function of respiration dynamically connects you to your world. At a more subtle level, this 'air' element is associated with the movement of subtle energies throughout the subtle energy systems of the body sometimes pictured in acupuncture or esoteric anatomy charts. On a macroscale, this element weaves the web of resonant energies which regulate the metabolism of the planet, and entrain and attune us with the movements of the heavens. Contemplate the pervasiveness of this air-wind element within and around you.

The faculty of awareness or knowingness is often associated with the most essential element. This most subtle element is not physical in nature. It is called by many names: consciousness, ether, mind, spirit, that which does not die, etc. This is the animating force unique to life, the vital essence that sees through our eyes, listens through our ears, and is ever awake and aware in the heart of all living beings.

The contemplation of these five elements is used in many traditions as a means of enabling individuals to better align themselves with the inner and outer elements of life and the cosmos.

15 *Hollow body meditation*

One of the most effective techniques for dissipating accumulated stress and tension is to experience your body as hollow, open and filled with clear space. Experience this space as neither solid nor empty, but rather as an inner openness within which feelings and sensations can freely come and go. This inner openness and spaciousness is devoid of any obstruction or any sense of solidity and denseness.

This deceptively simple method has been used for thousands of years and has recently been extensively documented to promote the integration and optimization of neuromuscular, autonomic and central nervous system functions, as well as to reduce pain, enhance endurance and overall mindbody coordination.

Begin by sitting comfortably with your spine straight and your body relaxed.

Now, bring your attention to the breath, and as you inhale imagine drawing your attention into your head. It may be helpful to imagine the breath like a luminous crystal mist that completely fills your head. As you breathe out, let go of the image or feeling of denseness or solidity and imagine this region as completely open and filled with space. Sense and feel the sensations and vibrations that come and flow freely within this open space inside your head.

As you next breathe in, draw your attention into your neck and throat, and again as you breathe out, imagine this region is left filled with space — a space open to the flow of life energy, vibration and sensation. Experience a sense of inner openness, a space free from denseness or solidity.

Continue now to breathe your awareness region by region into each part of your body. One region at a time, breathe this sense of luminous open space into your hands, arms and shoulders, your chest, abdomen, hips and buttocks and genitals, and finally your legs and feet. As you exhale, feel and vividly imagine that each region is left feeling utterly open to the flowing streams of sensation and vibration that knit the fabric of your experience. Amidst this flow of vibration and sensation, experience the inner quiet stillness and peacefulness that accommodates all these myriad changes and vibrations.

Now simply rest in this experience of your hollow body without conceptualization or analysis. Simple allow thoughts, feelings, perceptions and images to arise and dissolve like luminous bubbles and streams flowing within this inner space of awareness. Experience your body as unified and whole, completely open to equalizing and diffusing the accumulated pressures of your body and mind. Allow each breath to deepen this inner harmony and to energize the calm intensity of your awareness.

Initally you may find that some regions feel dense, solid and impregnable. You may be unable to get a clear feeling for these regions. Many people have cut themselves off from parts of their body due to past injuries, surgery, abuse as a child, or other conscious or suppressed trauma. So long as there are parts of your body cut off from your sense of wholeness, parts of your brain and mind potentials are blocked as well. These 'locked closets' of your body leave you vulnerable as they are often the breeding ground for degenerative disease and cancer. In this case, combine your practice of this technique with the *Mental massage* (page 137).

Gradually and with practice you will easily be able to imagine and actually feel that your whole body, from the top of your head to the tip of your toes is completely open, unobstructed, unified and radiant. This inner sense of your wholeness will enable you to reclaim those lost regions of your body, brain and mind. Eventually you will be able to access this unified, open and luminous sense of your entire body with a single breath.

Advanced variations

The following variations on the hollow body technique will further enhance your mindbody coordination and self healing abilities.

1. Having dissolved your whole body into a unified sphere of empty openness, imagine your body in different sizes. Gradually allow your sense of your body to grow smaller and smaller. Reduce it to the size of a sesame seed and then expand it until it contains the room, the building, the globe, the Milky Way and the universe. Take as much time as you need to vividly sense and flex these undeveloped capacities of your mind. Alternate between tiny and vast as you feel comfortable, maintaining a feeling of hollowness and luminous openness throughout.

2. Having become familar with this technique, proceed to the following variation. Allow your body to appear and feel hollow and radiant. Then expand your awareness to fill the universe. Next, gradually imagine the entire universe dissolving down to absorb into your body. Then imagine your body dissolving from top and bottom into a small sphere of light at the center of your chest. Imagine this tiny luminous sphere growing smaller and smaller until your mind simply dissolves into a lucid empty openness.

Now rest in this empty open space: still, quiet, clear, and non-conceptual. As the first thought arises in this stillness of your mind, immediately generate yourself as your hollow body again, yet this time feel as though all of your old limiting thoughts, negative habits of perception and behavior, and physical congestions have completely dissolved into space and that you are arising fresh, clean, clear, radiant and purified − in a sense reborn.

With frequent practice of these techniques the strength of

old limiting patterns will gradually diminish, allowing you to access more effective and creative responses to the opportunities and challenges of your life.

Carry-over practice

As you move throughout your day carry this inner sense of unified openness and wholeness with you. Frequently use the breath to help you renew this sense. To deepen and enhance the benefits of this technique, train your mind to pay attention to the space and distance between things, and to imagine and sense the volume and natural radiance of other people and objects. Notice how the spaces between buildings, cars, people and clouds actually connect everything. Train your inner and outer perception to experience how space, within and without, connects everything. With practice you will gradually come to attend to space and emptiness in relation to objects and things. You will learn to recognize space as a unifying medium rich in information of many frequencies and wavelengths transduced by our ordinary and subtle senses. This quality of sensitivity can further be enhanced by practicing listening for the silences between sounds, and noticing the space between thoughts. This is a necessary foundation for enhancing intuition and expanding the range of your subtle senses.

16 *Mental massage*

Massage the inside of your body with your mind. Sweep your attention through your body like a gentle breeze that moves from the inside out. Allow the mind to move deeply and unobstructedly throughout the body, as though everything inside you were openness and patterns of energy and space. Allow the attention to move particularly through regions of discomfort or disease. Gently direct the mind to sweep back and forth, up and down, moving like a laser beam or a flood light, sweeping from different directions, front to back, top to bottom, diagonally or in spirals. Intuitively feel how you can best move your attention into a region of internal space and try different approaches.

Pay particular attention to how these subtle sensations change, how everything inside you is moving, vibrating, changing moment to moment. If you have difficulty focusing your attention in this way, bring your attention to your breathing for a while and when your concentration has been energized return to this sweeping of mind through body.

Though at first you may work at the level of imagination, you can quickly develop the subtle, deep awareness which is able to sense, feel and actually alter patterns of subtle sensation, prephysical and electromagnetic energy through your conscious intention and attention. Though at first the body may seem riddled with discomfort or some regions may be impossible to sense or feel at all, gradually these parts of yourself will come alive with sensation and feeling of a more harmonious resonance.

While biomedical scientists elaborated mechanistic models of health and illness, the conceptual basis of their science was shattered by dramatic developments in atomic and subatomic physics, which clearly revealed the limitations of the mechanistic world view and lead to an organic and ecological conception of reality. In twentieth century physics, the universe is no longer perceived as a machine made up of a multitude of separate objects, but appears as a harmonious indivisible whole; a web of dynamic relationships that include the human observer and his or her consciousness in an essential way. Space and time are no longer separate dimensions, both are interwoven and form a four-dimensional continuum called spacetime. Subatomic particles are interconnections in a network of events, bundles of energy, or patterns of activity. When we observe them, we never see any material substance; what we observe are dynamic patterns continually changing into one continuous dance of energy.
Fritjof Capra

17 *The center of your mandala*

Sitting comfortably and at ease, breathe and draw the universe into you. Breathing out from the nucleus of your inner mandala, feel yourself sitting at the center of your universe. Imagine your sphere of energy and awareness opening to enfold and infuse the space around you.

Allow the flow of the breath to effortlessly remind you of your dynamic relationship with the universe. Remember that you are always at the center of your world, wherever you go. And remember that every single being likewise abides at the center of their own mandala. Interpenetrating spheres of energy and consciousness fill space with an intricate lattice work of mandalas generated from the nucleus of each atom and each being.

Each being embracing and embraced by all others.

Sit firm, confident and serene at the center of your mandala of energy and awareness.

And if any experience knocks you off center, simply breathe and draw yourself back to the center.

18 *The drop and the ocean*

Quietly and comfortably now, allow the breath to freely come and flow, effortlessly releasing and dissolving thoughts and tensions into space.

As you inhale, imagine a bubble of light energy filling you from within. As you exhale, imagine this bubble expanding...opening and expanding out into the space around you. With each breath, be filled by this luminous energy, and with each exhalation, imagine this sphere of light energy opening and expanding, moving freely through the space, the walls, the buildings, the earth around you. Let everything open. Let your small sense of self expand and open to your surroundings. Allow all of the feelings and sensations and vibrations within your body to expand, open and dissolve like a cloud melting into space. Use the breath to help you learn to expand your sphere of energy awareness like the expanding circle of a pebble dropped onto a still pool...ahhh...opening...opening... in all directions...filling the space above you, filling the space below you, expanding and opening out before you, behind you opening and expanding as a sphere of energy-life-awareness all around you...opening and expanding with each breath.

Now as you inhale, allow this light energy to take on a pleasing color and feeling-quality — perhaps blue and peaceful, or red and warm, or any color feeling combination that feels right to you. Allow this feeling and color to fill you deeply and then as you exhale, allow the color feeling sphere to open and expand within and around you. Imagine filling the space around you with luminous waves of warmth and well-being. Imagine generating an atmosphere of peace, of happiness and good vibrations that pervades the world around you. Sitting quietly, simply allow this well-spring of inner energy to come alive, open and expand around you so that anyone near you can receive the benefit.

Now, having established this expansive sense of well-being, imagine that as your sphere of energy awareness opens and expands, there is an echo from the universe at large. Imagine that as your drop or nucleus of energy expands outwards, a vast ocean of peace, of warmth, and of love converges and pours into you. Simultaneously now, experience this feeling of expansion and convergence. Your tiny mind drop opening outwards, and dissolving into a vast spacious ocean, and this ocean of positive energy vibration flowing, and converging into your drop. Allow all of your limitations, pains, thoughts and cares to be dissolved into this free flowing convergence.

Variation

This is an excellent technique for dissolving emotional pain as well.

As you exhale, allow the energy or feeling of the pain to open out and dissolve into space. As the energy vibration of the pain expands, sense or vividly imagine feeling a healing echo of energy-vibration pouring into you from the energy-ocean surrounding you. Feel this healing wave flowing into you and dissolving into the region of the pain. For example, when you experience a sense of burning, allow that feeling to expand while simultaneously, a cool, soothing energy is drawn back into you. If you are feeling agitated, allow that feeling to open, expand and dissipate while at the same time you feel deep peace pouring into you, flooding you completely with well-being. Allow yourself to receive from the universe-at-large whatever you most need at this time.

Breathing out, give yourself permission to let go of the knots of tension that block your body, fog your mind and block your heart. Let everything within you open into harmony. Allow the breath to naturally and effortlessly bathe your tissues in oxygen and light that dissolves the tensions or pains. Allow the waves of breath to fill you with the love, the courage and the strength that you need to let go of tension, to let go of fear, to release doubt, or anger and to rest in your own wholeness.

Breathing and receiving what you need...releasing the old limitations...resting in wholeness...tune into whatever frequency of positive healing qualities that you need at this time...

19 *Transforming emotions*

Ordinarily our emotional responses are highly conditioned and automatic. Blown by the winds of our emotions, we often experience confusion, disharmony and physical disease. Once you understand this process, you can assume more control and responsibility for how you use your emotions. You can learn to regain your balance and bring harmony to your mindbody by generating appropriate emotions as an antidote to the self-centered and often destructive aspects of your emotional reactions.

In order to work on transforming our emotional reactions, it is necessary to first understand how emotions work. One way to approach this is with the following model. Here we have four basic emotional states followed by their potentially dark side. Each of these eight basic emotions are interrelated. In each, the emotional feeling shown in capital letters is the more matured state, expressing the true and natural human

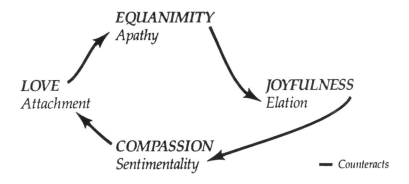

being. The emotional feeling that is indicated in small letters is the condition that you may slip into if the experience becomes tinged with self-centeredness. One is the manifestation of the true and free spark of human intelligence and the other is the self-centered, egoistic aspect that it can easily become:

EQUANIMITY can lead to apathy,
JOYFULNESS to elation,
COMPASSION to sentimentality,
LOVE to attachment.

Meditation training helps you to focus your attention to understand the interplay of mental attitudes, emotional feelings and physical reactions. As you come to understand this complex process you can maintain or restore your internal balance by generating an emotion that is an appropriate antidote to a disturbing emotional state. For instance:

LOVE counteracts apathy,
EQUANIMITY will ground you from elation,
JOYFULNESS will melt your fixation on sentimentality,
COMPASSION will inhibit attachment.

If you are bored, let yourself love someone you love beyond that individual to others who may need to feel loved.

If your compassion is dissipated into sentimentality, rejoice a little, and if you become too elated, generate more equanimity to calm down.

Remember, each of our emotions can be expressed from the true essence of the human spirit or from a distorted bias of our own self-centeredness. One will set you free, while the other will perpetually entrap you in a cycle of disharmony.

Other strategies for transforming emotions include

1. In an emotionally charged situation, focus your attention on the physical sensations in your body and on your own emotional feelings — not on the situation or on those

involved. If you feel tension, holding or squeezing in your body, bring your attention to those feelings. Breathe... and relax. Remember you are the only one responsible for your mental, emotional and physical response to the situation. Breathe, relax and open your field of attention to find a creative solution or response to the challenge.

2. Investigate the physical sensations and mental images related to your emotional state. Reflect, 'What does this fear, anger, sadness or grief really feel like? Where do I feel it in my body? How big is it? Where does it come from or go to? What are the thoughts and mental tape loops associated with this emotional state?' You will find that by simply investigating the nature of your emotional reactions, the intensity will diminish. You will be able to calm and clear your mind and to respond from a state of centered strength.

3. When you feel overwhelmed by other people's pain, let that pain tear your heart open. Awaken genuine compassion: compassion for the difficulties and suffering or helplessness; compassion for your own frustration or helplessness; compassion for all others who might feel as they or you feel in that situation.

4. When others act cruelly or insensitively, remember that no one can act that way unless they are suffering themselves. The more quickly you are able to recognize and transform your own negative emotional patterns the less likely you are to hurt someone else.

5. Think about the irony of being angry about feeling angry, or guilty about feeling guilty. Learning to recognize and accept old conditioned emotional reactions is the first step to changing them.

6. Learn to befriend your confused or negative emotions. When a negative emotion arises, smile to yourself and mentally note, 'Ah, anger (or blame, guilt, or jealousy)...of course!'

7. Develop a flexibility of emotional response. In the face of anger, for example, practice generating compassion towards yourself and others. In the face of greed, practice

generating gratitude for all that you have. Experiencing jealousy, try finding the feeling of rejoicing in the good fortune of another. When impatient, practice patience.

8. When all else fails, learn from your mistakes! Analyze the situation after it's over, clarify how you might improve your response in the future and vividly imagine yourself in a similar situation responding the way that you would like to.

As you develop the ability to authentically recognize and acknowledge what you are feeling you will be better able to understand the destructive potential of negative emotional states. This direct understanding will enable you to consciously cultivate new and more effective emotional responses which bring greater balance and harmony to your mindbody, your behavior and relationships.

20 *Meditation on forgiveness*

As we develop in our practice of meditation we naturally become more conscious of what is going on in our own minds. We become clearer about what we feel and why. We start to uncover the discrepancies in our lives, and get in touch with the bruises and hurts of old relationships. Slowly, we are able to tie loose ends and heal the wounds.

The practice of a forgiveness meditation is a wonderful way to heal the pain of the old hurts that block our heart and prevent us from trusting and loving ourselves and others. Forgiveness is the key to opening our hearts, to learning from the painful lessons of the past in order to move into the future unhindered.

Begin by sitting quietly, relaxing your body and focusing your mind with the breath. Allow memories and images and emotions to float freely in your mind — things you have done, said and thought that you have not forgiven yourself for, no matter how painful they are.

From your heart say to yourself, 'I forgive myself for whatever I have done in the past, intentionally or unintentionally, my actions, my words and my thoughts. I have suffered enough! I have learned and grown and I am ready now to open my heart to myself. May I be happy, may I be free from confusion, may I know the joy of truly understanding myself, others and the world. May I come to know my own wholeness and fullness and help others to do the same.'

Now, in the space in front of you, imagine a person you love whom you want to forgive or whose forgiveness you need. From your heart to theirs directly communicate the following: 'With all my heart I forgive you for whatever you may have done, intentionally or unintentionally, by your actions, your words or thoughts that have caused me pain. I forgive you, and I ask that you forgive me for whatever I have done, intentionally or unintentionally to you, by my actions, my words or my thoughts. I ask your forgiveness. May you be happy, free and joyful. May we both open our hearts and minds to meet in love and understanding as we grow into wholeness.' Imagine that this message is received and accepted, and affirm the feeling of healing between you. Then let the image melt into space.

Now, in the space in front of you imagine someone toward whom you feel great resentment or negativity. To the best of your ability and from your heart to theirs, communicate the essence of the following: 'From my heart I forgive you for whatever you have done, intentionally or unintentionally, that has caused me pain. I forgive you for the actions and words and thoughts that you have expressed from your own pain, confusion, insensitivity and fear of me. I forgive you, and I ask that you forgive me for the way in which I have intentionally or unintentionally closed my heart to you. I ask your forgiveness for causing you suffering. May you be happy. May you be free from suffering and confusion. May we both open our hearts to meet in love and understanding as we grow into our wholeness.' Imagine that this message has been received and accepted, and affirm the healing that has taken place within you and between the two of you. Then allow the image to melt into space.

Next, think about the countless people toward whom you have closed your heart. Remember how you felt and what you did when people abused you, spoke harshly, took 'your' parking place, crowded in front of you in line, ad infinitum . . . Consider how many people you have hurt in some way, by your own conscious or unconscious actions, words and thoughts. How many times have *you* been the abuser, the one who crowded in, the one who spoke harshly? Imagine these countless beings standing before you. From your heart to theirs generate the essence of the following: 'I forgive you for whatever you have done, intentionally or unintentionally that has caused me to suffer. I forgive you and ask you to forgive me for whatever I have done, intentionally or un-intentionally, that has hurt you. May you and I and all of us create the causes for happiness in our lives. May we out-grow and transform the causes of our suffering. May we all come to know the joy of truly understanding and experi-encing our interrelationship. May we open our hearts and minds to each other and meet in harmony.

Repeat this reflective meditation as often as you like. At the conclusion, imagine and feel as vividly and wholeheartedly as you are able that you have actually released all guilt and blame towards yourself. In this present moment, allow yourself to feel forgiveness and a patient acceptance of your past actions.

21 Increasing compassion

The following meditation is taken from a talk given by the Dalai Lama.

'Avoid harming others and whenever possible be of service.'

If you wish to increase your compassion, you can think in this way. First visualize yourself as a neutral person. Now, on the right side, visualize your old self as a person who is only ever seeking his or her own welfare, who doesn't think at all about other people, who would take advantage of anyone at any time whenever the chance arises, and who is never content. And, on the left side of your neutral self, visualize a group of people who are really suffering and need some help.

Now think: all humans have the natural desire to be happy and to avoid suffering: all humans equally have the right to be happy and to get rid of suffering. Then think in a wise, not selfish way: everybody wants happiness, nobody wants to be foolish or to be like that selfish person.

So you see, if we want to be a good person, a more reasonable, logical person, then we don't want to be like the narrow-minded selfish person on the right. We wouldn't want to join this single, selfish , greedy, discontented person on the right. If we were to draw a line between the single selfish person and the group, you would want to join the group.

When we practice this technique of visualization, naturally the majority side wins our heart. The closer you come to taking the side of the majority, the further you become from your selfishness. Because you yourself are the meditator, your own sense of altruism will increase and increase. If you practice this way daily, it will be helpful.

The hardest state to be in is one in which you keep your heart open to the suffering that exists around you, and simultaneously keep your discriminative wisdom. It's for easier to do one or the other; to keep your heart open and get lost into pity, empathetic suffering, righteous indignation, etc.; or remain remotely detached as a witness to it all. Once you understand that true compassion is the blending of the open heart and the quiet mind, it is still difficult to find the balance. Most often we start out doing these things sequentially. We open our hearts and get lost into the melodramas, then we meditate and regain our quiet centre by pulling back in from so much openness. Then we once again open and get sucked back into the dance. So it goes cycle after cycle.

It takes a good while to get the balance. For at first the discriminative awareness part of the cycle makes you feel rather like a cold fish. You feel as if you have lost your tenderness and caring. And yet each time you open again to the tender emotions, you get lost into the drama and see your predicament: if you really want to help others who are suffering, you just have to develop the balance between heart and mind such that you remain soft and flowing yet simultaneously clear and spacious. You have to stay right on the edge of that balance. It seems impossible, but you do it. At first, when you achieve this balance, it is self-consciously maintained. Ultimately, however, you merely become the statement of the amalgam of the open heart and quiet mind. Then there is no more struggle; it's just the way you are.

Ram Dass

22 *Loving kindness meditation*

This meditation was inspired by B. Alan Wallace.

Relax the body, take three deep breaths and continue briefly with the awareness of the natural respiration.

From the relative serenity and calmness of the mind, let's engage in the reflective meditation of the cultivation of loving kindness. In this practice we focus initially upon ourselves, recognizing the unwholesome behavior to which we are still prone, the mental distortions to which we are still subject, and yet recognizing that at our very core lies this essential purity, that the mind is essentially untainted. There is a potential here that is fathomless, a potential for wisdom and compassion; and our very wish for well-being, for happiness, our very wish to be free of suffering may be regarded as an expression of that true nature. Let it be unveiled, allowing it to manifest its full potential. From that perspective, acknowledging the shortcomings, the unwholesome traits, and behavior patterns, cultivate the prayer, cultivate the aspiration, the wish: may I be free of these distortions, free of anger, free of grasping, free of confusion, free of arrogance. May I be free of the mental suffering that ensues from such distortions of the mind. And may I recognize and cultivate those other qualities of my present being, of loving kindness and compassion, of wisdom and patience — the whole array of wholesome qualities that are there too. And for my own well-being and the well-being of others, may these arise, may these flourish. And may I experience the wonderful sense of well-being, and a wholesome way of life, from the profound stabilization of the mind, from deep compassion and from deep insight. In that way, may I be well and happy. May my fears and sorrows

fall away. May I find a joy that is untainted by anxiety, a joy that is not precarious, that is not balancing on a few pleasant stimuli or fortunate circumstances, but a joy that comes from my own heart. And imagine this to be so, as vividly, as realistically as you can. Imagine this to be so right now.

Bring to mind a loved one, a person whom you respect and love, a person such that when you see him or her, the immediate response is one of gladness, spontaneous gladness and affection. And this person, like myself, probably has shortcomings as well, is subject to unwholesome activity, to mental distortions; but this person, like myself, is endowed with the true nature, has the complete capacity for full spiritual awakening. This person, like myself, wishes to be free of sorrow and to experience true joy and happiness. May this person, like myself, become ever freer of the mental distortions, unwholesome behavior, and of the sorrow, the conflict, the suffering that ensue from them. And may this person find those wholesome qualities and cultivate them by whatever path carries them to their goals. May this person find his or her own path, one that most effectively nourishes this person. And for the growth of these wholesome qualities, for the unveiling of this person's true nature, may this person, like myself, be truly well and happy, free of suffering, free of unnecessary suffering and grief; and imagine it to be so, as vividly as you can.

Focus now on someone you simply feel indifferent toward. It might be a grocery clerk you see frequently, or a person at a gas station, or a colleague, a person you work with, for whom you have no special feeling at all. And recognize that this person too, like myself, is endowed with the true nature, like myself, feels suffering and feels joy. This person may have no kind of spiritual orientation at all, but the experience of suffering and joy is no less real, no less important. So, like myself, may this person cultivate those wholesome qualities and subdue the unwholesome and may this person, like myself, be well and happy, free of unnecessary pain and grief and fear. And imagine it to be so.

And finally take a person that you really don't like, a person whom you'd just rather not see at all, not hear at all, not even hear about. Perhaps this person has wronged you or perhaps it is simply personality characteristics in that person that you disdain. And recognize that what we are identifying here are those very distortions, those very unwholesome types of activity that are the source of sorrow, that this person is subject to them like I am, perhaps in a grosser way, but these are the afflictions. And as it is unrealistic and not useful to identify with my own shortcomings, likewise not to identify another person with that person's shortcomings, distortions, afflictions. Recognize that that person, like myself, wishes to be happy, wishes to be free of sorrow. Maybe the ways of pursuing this are confused, but the wish is no less real, the experience of joy and sorrow is no less real. And if this person were to find effective means for subduing unhappiness, for rooting out the sources of unnecessary grief and conflict, the very reasons why I am adverse to that person would vanish and there would be a lovely person emerging in that person's place. With that perspective, it is not hard to aspire: may this person, like myself, be well and happy. May those afflications fall away. May this person's True Nature be unveiled and the beauty of this person emerge. Imagine it to be so.

As we bring the meditation to a close, let's allow such a quality of awareness to express itself also in form by imagining a pearl of radiant white light of the nature of purity, of the nature of loving kindness which is of the very essence of one's own True Nature. Imagine this pearl of radiant, brilliant, white light at the heart and from an inexhaustible source, allow that light to suffuse every cell of your body, thoroughly saturating the body with this light, this light of loving kindness, of purity and purification.

And then imagine the body being so filled that it is no longer able to contain this light, but rays of light emerge in all directions, in front and in back, to the left and right, upwards and downwards — in all directions. An inexhaustible source of light flows forth in all directions as an expression of your loving kindness, of your loving concern for all beings who, like yourself, aspire for happiness and wish to be free from suffering. Imagine these rays of light touching individuals all about us in this neighborhood, in this city, illuminating the environment and bringing well-being, bringing food where there is poverty and starvation, rain where there is drought, harmony where there is conflict, and peace where there is hatred. And let that light expand around the entire globe and beyond.

In this way, we can dedicate the merit, we can dedicate the spiritual power of this practice, not just to our own isolated well-being, our own individual well-being, but dedicate it, direct it to the well-being, the peace of the entire world, of all beings without exception. In this way we give all that we have, and we receive even more in return.

If you should close your meditation session at least once a day with this, it will add a greater dimension to your whole practice. It will be of greater benefit to you and the people that you come in contact with.

23 *The four immeasurable attitudes*

In this practice one cultivates the contemplation of immeasurably vast love, compassion, sympathetic joy and
equanimity, and extends these towards all living beings
throughout the vastness of time and space.

Consider *love* as the wish that all beings be happy,
compassion as the wish that all be free from suffering,
sympathetic joy as an attitude that rejoices in the good fortune of others, and *equanimity* as an attitude of impartiality
(not indifference) that regards all beings as essentially equal.

Begin by generating the immeasurably vast attitude of
equanimity by recognizing the essential equality and
similarity of all beings. Consider how everyone wishes to
have happiness and well-being as well as to avoid suffering
and pain. Now, in a boundless way extend the thought: 'If
all beings were to live in an immeasurable equanimity even
minded and open hearted to all, how wonderful that would
be! May all beings come to abide in this even minded and
open hearted state by realizing their essential equality! I will
realize this essential equality of all beings and help others to
do the same.'

Generating an immeasurably vast attitude of love, consider
how you yourself and all others wish for happiness. In a
boundless way extend the thought: 'If all beings were happy
and had the causes for happiness, how wonderful that
would be! May they come to have this happiness, and may I
develop the ability to bring them to happiness.'

Generating an immeasurably vast attitude of compassion,

consider the many kinds of suffering, pain and disease experienced by different types of people and other living creatures. In a boundless way extend the wish: 'If all beings were free from suffering and the causes of suffering, how wonderful it would be! May they come to be free from their suffering, and may I develop the wisdom and power to be able to free them.'

Generating an immeasurably vast attitude of sympathetic joy, consider the positive potentials of all beings. In a boundless way extend the thought: 'If all beings were to know the joy of understanding and realizing all their positive potentials how wonderful that would be. May they come to realize everything that is wonderful! I will help them to realize the causes of true joy!'

Once you have a feeling for the practice, simply allow your mind to settle deeply into the contemplation of each of these qualities. One by one, imagine your love, compassion, rejoicing and even minded, open heartedness filling the vastness of space extending to all beings everywhere.

24 The practice of giving and taking

Throughout most of our lives we have been preoccupied with ensuring our own happiness and comfort. This self-cherishing attitude has trained our mind to grasp at pleasure and push away pain, and often to neglect reaching out to others with the heartfelt understanding that they are just like ourselves.

This meditation on *giving* happiness and *taking* pain is a powerful and effective method for training the mind to reach out to others in a more meaningful, healing and helpful way. It is not easy to imagine taking on the suffering of others, so it is good to start by absorbing and transforming our own difficulties and pains.

To begin, do the hollow body meditation (page 133). Once it is firmly established, allow *all* your feelings, sensations, visions, thoughts and other experiences to freely come and flow without resistance or attachment. Be aware of your breath flowing in and out. Then, imagine a black hole at your heart center. As you inhale, draw into this black hole all your mental and physical pain, visualized as black smoke, and imagine that it totally dissolves and disappears.

Now, imagine that the hole is white. As you exhale, visualize wave upon wave of clear, radiant light blazing forth from your heart center and completely filling your body and mind, healing, energizing and transforming you.

Next, extend this to include all your negativities of the rest of today, tomorrow, next week, next year... Completely accept them into your heart center as black smoke, and then radiate out pure, clear light, immeasurably enhancing your capacity for health, happiness and wisdom.

After practicing taking on your own suffering for several sessions, you may feel ready to visualize taking on the suffering of others — the prime object of this meditation technique.

By utilizing the inhalation and exhalation of the breath, the practice becomes easier. First we inhale, breathing slowly and calmly, generating the intention to accept the suffering of others. This comes in the form of dark fumes entering with the breath and absorbing into us. Then, with the motivation to give all our own happiness to others in order to alleviate their suffering, we generate from within ourselves pure white light radiating from our hearts and flowing out through our nostrils. This radiant light spreads out in all directions to fill space and time, giving to every being whatever it is they most need in order to be happy.

Perhaps you may wonder how this practice can actually benefit anyone, for even though we visualize that we are taking on the suffering of others, no apparent changes seem to have taken place in those around us. Our happiness does not seem to go anywhere and the suffering of others is not noticeably alleviated.

However, the point is that 'giving and taking' in this way trains and develops our own mind. By doing this practice we break through our habitual patterns of grasping at our own happiness and being indifferent to the suffering of others. And it is this mental development that helps us reach the state of realization in which all obstacles have been transformed and all positive qualities have been completely matured within our continuum.

Gradually, we develop our mind until it is fully compassionate, powerful and wise — until it is fully awakened. At that point, it will be possible to realize our wish to truly help others.

25 *Meditation on the teacher*

*Do not believe in what you have heard; do not
believe in the traditions because they have been
handed down for generations; do not believe in
anything because it is rumoured or spoken by many;
do not believe merely because a written statement of
some old sage is produced; do not believe in
conjectures; do not believe in that as truth to which
you have become attached by habit; do not believe
merely the authority of your teachers and elders.
After observation and analysis, when it agrees with
reason and is conducive to the goods and gain of one
and all, then accept it, practice it and live up to it.*
The Budda

This meditation is taken from Silent Mind, Holy Mind *by
Lama Thubten Yeshe*
As a daily practice, you could do the following. Sit, or
kneel if you like, in a comfortable position, relaxed but with
your back straight. In you mind's eye, visualize Jesus (or any
other great teacher or spiritual friend) before you. His face
has a tranquil, peaceful and loving expression. A picture of
the resurrected Christ or of Jesus teaching may be used as a
model for this visualization.

Then visualize from the crown of his head radiant, white light coming to your own crown. This white light is in the nature of blissful energy and as it enters your body it purifies the physical contamination, or sin, accumulated over countless lifetimes. This blissful, white energy purifies all diseases of the body, including cancers, and activates and renews the functioning of your entire nervous system.

In a similar manner, red light is visualized radiating forth from Jesus' throat and entering your own, completely pervading your vocal center with the sensation of bliss. If you have difficulties with your speech — always telling lies, being uncontrolled in what you say, engaging in slander, using harsh language or the like — this blissful red energy purifies you of all these negativities. As a result you discover the divine qualities of speech.

Then from Jesus' heart, infinite radiant blue light comes to sink into your heart, purifying your mind of all its wrong conceptions. Your selfish and petty ego, which is like the chief or president of the delusions, and the three poisons of greed, hatred and ignorance, which are like the ego's ministers, are all purified in this blissful, blue radiance. The indecisive mind, which is especially doubtful and caught between 'maybe this' and 'maybe that' is clarified. Also purified is the narrow mind, which cannot see the totality because its focus is too tight. As the light energy fills your mind, your heart becomes like the blue sky, embracing universal reality and all of space.

This three-part purification of body, speech and mind can be very helpful for anyone having great devotion to Jesus. If you are unable to visualize all of the above, you can concentrate merely on Jesus' heart. From this center very blissful, white radiant energy comes to you heart, purifying all defilements. This is a simplified practice, but still can be extremely helpful.

You can conclude this meditation by visualizing a white lotus flower blooming in your heart. The compassionate figure visualized in front of you then sinks into your heart and manifests on this lotus seat. Afterwards, whatever you eat or drink becomes an offering to this Jesus within your heart. If this meditation is done daily with good concentration and a pure motivation, it can be very effective in transforming your ordinary actions, words and thoughts and in bringing you closer to the divine qualities of Jesus.

Silent meditation, without thought, totally open,
awake and aware, this is absolute prayer!
Lama Thubten Yeshe

26 *Mother of compassion*

The following meditation was told to John Blofeld by an old woman, a nun, in Canton.

You sit down on a hill top, or anywhere high enough
  for you to see nothing but the sky in front of your eyes
With your mind you make everything empty.

  There is nothing there you say.
And you see it like that — nothing
                emptiness.
                    Then you say ahhh...
      But there IS something!
    Look there's the sea
    and the MOON has risen
      full, round, white.

And you see it like that
        sea, silver in the moonlight
      with little white topped waves.
    And in the blue black sky above
    hangs a great moon
      bright,
        but not dazzling,
        a soft brightness you might say.

You stare at the moon a long
  long time, feeling calm, happy.
      Then the moon gets smaller,
        but brighter and brighter and brighter
till you see it as a pearl, or a seed, but so bright
      you can only just bear to look at it.

The pearl starts to grow.
   And before you know what's happened,
        it's Kuan Yin (the Mother of Compassion) herself
     standing up against the sky
     all dressed in gleaming white
       and with her feet resting on a lotus
         that floats on the waves.

You see her
   once you know how to do it
as clearly as I see you.
Her robes are shining,
    and there's a halo round her head.
     She smiles at you,
        such a loving smile. She's so glad
to see you that tears of happiness sparkle in her eyes.
       If you keep your mind calm,
by just whispering her name
and not trying too hard
she will stay a long time.

When she does go,
    it's by getting smaller and smaller.
    She doesn't go back to being a pearl,
       but just gets so small
       that at last you can't see her, then you notice
that the sky and sea
have vanished too.
       Just space is left.
Lovely, lovely space, going on forever...

      that space stays long
if you can do without *you*. Not *you* and space, you see

    just space.

    No you!

27 *Sphere of light*

Sitting quietly now with your eyes closed or slightly open, imagine a luminous sphere of light, like the sun, shining in the space in front and above you. Let this sphere be an idealized representation of all the mental, physical, emotional and spiritual qualities that you most wish to energize and embody in your life at this time. Vividly imagine that you are soaking up all the rays of this light source and its energy of relaxation, calm, clarity and inner strength, as though you were sunbathing. Feel these rays soaking into you, pervading your body and mind — more deeply and completely with each breath. Let these feelings of calmness, inner strength and harmony grow and glow deeply within you.

Now imagine that this shining luminous sphere sends light tendrils out to all corners of the universe, to all the sources of inspiration, healing and harmonizing energy that you need at this time. Imagine these rays of light drawing back into this sphere all the healing and harmonizing power that exists throughout space and time. It all pours back into your shining sphere of light, charging it up into a crystal that showers you with the light of a billion shining suns. Now imagine this brilliant light energy streaming into you, completely dissolving all your tensions and pains, all your worries and cares, healing and opening the places in your body, heart and mind that need to become whole. Feel the inner clouds of darkness vanishing in this flood of brilliant light. Feel the fog of sluggishness and dullness dissolve completely into a vitalized calm within.

Imagine this shining sphere of light coming closer now, pouring its light down into you. Let it come to the top of your head. Feel a shower of cleansing, healing, purifying light flooding you, washing you completely clean and clear throughout. Vividly imagine your body as a crystal flooded with rainbow light. Now imagine this light pouring through you, shining through your eyes, from your heart, through the pores of your skin. Flowing out into the world. Tidal waves of healing, helpful, crystal rainbow-like light shining to you. Flowing through you and into the world.

Now, if you like, imagine this luminious sphere coming down into you like a glorious brilliant nova of powerful rainbow light slipping into a crystal sea, merging and melting into the luminous open space within you. Imagine that it transforms your body and mind into a vast open state of unimpeded clarity and luminosity, and that your emotions are transformed into those of power, harmony, generosity and confidence.

Experience yourself as a radiant being. Feel this deep vital energy pouring deeply through you and out into the world. Experience the peaceful power of this way of seeing yourself. Imagine that these waves of positive feeling are like clear rainbow light that can reach out to others in ways that bring relief, inspiration, energy or whatever else they may need. Wherever you direct your attention, let there be benefit.

28 Mantra: protection for the mind

Through the parallelism of body, mind and speech,
the coordination of movement, thought and word, the
harmony of feeling, creative imagination,
visualization and verbal expression, we achieve a
unity of all the functions of our conscious being,
which not only affects the surface of our personality
— namely our senses and our intellect — but equally
the deeper regions of our mind. In the regular
performance of such ritual worship, the very
foundations of our being are slowly but certainly
transformed and made receptive for the inner light.
Lama Govinda

One day, as a young boy, when I was in the synagogue
with my grandfather, a very old and pious man came over
to say hello. He had always caught my eye as being a uni-
quely calm and wise looking fellow, and as he approached
he seemed to be mumbling serenely to himself. Coming to
stand in front of us, his moving lips vocalized, 'The Lord is
good' in Hebrew, he had a short chat with Gramps, all the
while inaudibly chanting this phrase or mantra over and
over behind and between his words. His final audible
words to us were the same as his first, and as he left he
seemed to glide on this mantric wave as a continuum of
steadiness and balance for his mind.

Over the years, I've been introduced to the use of mantra or chanting in every meditative tradition that I've studied. The actual word mantra means 'mind protection.' That is to say that while one is engaged in chanting a mantra, one's mind is protected from disappointing its clarity and power in random or negative thoughts. In many meditative traditions, formal periods of quiet contemplative practice are preceeded by a time of devotional chanting or mantric repetition. The repetitive and often sacred nature of these chants can have a calming and stabilizing effect which builds coherence and power in the mind and the subtle nervous system.

The use of such 'mind protectors' is an old sacred science. The inner scientist knows and understands the use of sound and vibration as a tool to evoke and refine specific qualities of mind. In Native American traditions a young man or woman would be sent on a vision quest and told to listen for a sacred gong or death chant that the Great Spirit would teach to them during this time of alert receptive vigilance. After days of fasting, prayer or other ordeals, a chant would emerge into awareness as a gift or sign from the Great Spirit. From that time on, this death chant would be used to steady and protect the mind at critical times in one's life. Having practiced this chant in the face of adversity millions of times over the course of one's life, one would turn to it wholeheartedly and single-pointedly as one approached the moment of death, allowing it to carry one across the threshold between worlds and into the vastness of Spirit.

In the Tibetan tradition, the repetition of the mantras OM MANI PEDME HUNG, OM AH HUNG VAJRA GURU PEDME SIDDHI HUNG, and OM TARE TUTTARE TURE SVAHA are commonly recited one hundred thousand to one hundred million times in the course of one's life. The subtle psychophysical repetition of such mantric practice provides one with a coherent internal resonance that pervades one's mindbody as well as a continual sense of direct connection with the source of spiritual blessings, power and inspiration. The power of mantras, some say, is related to the cumulative effect of countless conscious repetitions over millenia of their use. By chanting a mantra one's mindbody sympathetically resonates with the cosmic reservoir of its accumulated power and if properly receptive one will experience an infusion of the blessing-energy of that particular mantra.

Clincially I've introduced this meditative practice to people who need to quiet and gentle their minds, with pregnant women and dying patients and loved ones. A friend who is an anesthesiologist often chants mantras in his patients ears as they drift off on the anesthetic. Throughout a pregnancy, a woman or couple can chant a mantra or sing a song of particular beauty or feeling for them. Gradually the fetus will become imbued with this familiar resonance. After birth, this can be chanted to them as a lullaby of reassurance, reducing the trauma of the birth transition. It can also be taught to other members of the family and baby sitters as a sound of comfort from across the room. Children will often respond in an alert and responsive way to these familiar sounds from their time in the womb.

The mantra OM MANI PEDME HUNG has been a final lullaby easing the transition of death for many special loved ones and friends. In the last days of their life, when there wasn't much to say in words, the gentle audible presence of this or other mantras effectively brought balance to their minds as they moved to subtler and subtler states of consciousness.

One of my wisest and kindest teachers, a true master of meditation who has spent nearly a third of his 82 years in various contemplative retreats, is continually chanting mantras as he directs his attention and intention of blessing towards countless beings. Used in this way, repetition of mantra is mental target practice in which all living beings are the targets of a heartfelt intention which is projected and carried by the mantra. Christian practioners might chant the name of Jesus or HALLELUYA, Hebrew practitioners the Shema or SHALOM, Sufi's the Zikar, others might work with OM, LOVE, PEACE, JOY ad infinitum. Though there *is* power in the actual vibration and sound of traditional mantras, the mental intention in its use determines the power and magnitude of its benefit.

The actual practice of mantra meditation can be quite simple. You can just sit quietly and mentally recite a mantra or meaningful phrase, resting the mind upon its sound or inner resonance within you. Whenever your mind wanders, simply return to the repetition and keep your attention on what you are doing. To elaborate on this method, visualize waves of light and good vibrations pouring from your heart to others, bringing more light, love and happiness into the world, and dissolving the darkness, pain and fear that fills the minds of so many beings.

When you have a feeling for it, working with mantra can help to calm and focus the mind when you are busy in the world. It is a simple, effective method for strengthening and developing positive qualities of the mind in moments that are ordinarily wasted − driving to work, waiting in line, holding the line on a telephone, walking down the street, and so on − all ordinary activities can be easily integrated into your meditation practice.

The practice of the inner essence of the mind protection is more a state of mind than a vocalization. In its deepest essence, it is a state of heart and mind that recognizes the non-duality and interdependent relationship of all beings and things. The response to this is the wisdom that spontaneously wishes to contribute to the well-being of others. This can be demonstrated not only through kind words and helpful actions, but through a resonance of heart and mind that reaches out to others in a deep, quiet and loving way.

When the mind is busy or directed towards superficial appearances, simply chanting a mantra with the intention of creating a more positive atmosphere in the world within and around you can be very helpful. As your mind becomes more subtle and quiet, the repetition of the mantra may likewise become subtler and subtler, until you rest in its innermost essence — silent prayer, a way of simply being natural that brings peace to the world within and around you. In this way, mantra and spoken prayer merge into silence and become the prayer of the heart.

29 *Meditations with a partner*

From every human being there arises a light that
reaches straight to heaven. And when two souls
destined to be together find each other, there streams
of light flow together and a single, brighter light goes
forth from their united being.
Baal Shem Toy
Renaissance Jewish mystic

Sharing meditation time can be a powerful means of bringing
depth and aliveness to our relationships. Meditating with a
partner provides an opportunity to let our conceptual and
emotional dust clear in order to see each other clearly,
freshly and in the ever unfolding newness of each moment.
Though an entire volume could be devoted to the intricacies
and delicacies of these 'dyadic' meditations, I'll briefly describe some ideas or techniques that you might enjoy sharing
and exploring with a special friend.

1. *Attunement*

Sit across from your partner palm to palm with your left
hands facing upwards and your right hands facing downwards. Take a few moments to breathe, relax, clear and open
your minds. As you breathe begin to establish and energize
a sense of your center of energy, awareness and heart-
fulness. Using your breathing, begin to extend a field or
sphere of these feelings and vibrations around you as you

envelop your partner. Simultaneously sense and allow the field and presence of your partner to be ever more deeply within and around you. Allow your fields of luminously charged awareness to blend into a field of sympathetic and harmonious resonance as though your two notes were reaching out to merge into a chord of shared awareness.

2. *Breath synchrony*

a) While one partner sits quietly in meditation, the other partner brings attention to the rhythm of the sitting partner's breathing. Gradually allow yourself to come into synch with their breathing. Coming into resonance, empathize.

b) This time simultaneously bring your attention to each other's breathing. Gradually allow your rhythms of inhaling and exhaling to come together. Let this shared attunement bring you into greater harmony and understanding at deeper and deeper levels.

3. *Giving and receiving*

Alternate inhalations and exhalations with your partner. Imagine breathing out love, energy, light or healing energy to your partner as your partner breathes that in. As you breathe in allow yourself to receive whatever quality of heart or mind they send to you. Let this method teach you about how you can open your heart and mind to both give and receive more generously.

4. *Merging hearts and minds*

With your partner, contemplate and feel the denseness and solidity of your bodies. Next shift your attention to a subtler body of energy, vibration and movement within this dense and solid form. At an even subtler level, sense an inner openness, spaciousness and boundlessness, like a vast inner sky that pervades your whole form and energy patterning.

In the dimension of form we merge sexually. In the dimension of energy and vibration we communicate and sense resonance, disonance and emotions. In the dimension of our openness we are of one essence interpenetrating and pervading all and sharing an open space of mind.

Within this matrix of form-energy-space, establish a nucleus or center of love and luminously positive feelings. From this center you might physically reach out to your partner with a physical caress, a kind word. At the level of vibration, your communication may be as a luminous wave of love and caring. Imagine and sense the possibility of your spheres of energy and space merging and interpenetrating. Though your bodies occupy distinct spaces, imagine what it would feel like if your spheres of energy and openness could interpenetrate. Allow your centers to merge and your fields of energy and awareness to become completely shared. Intimately feel within each other. From your heart fill your partner with love and offer energy to them to use as they most need it at this time. From your hearts share the flow of unspoken yet profoundly intimate communication springing from the depths of your hearts and minds. After a while gradually breathe your awareness back into its ordinary form-energy-space matrix and rejoice in the deep intimate sense of unity and wholeness that you have shared.

This is an excellent meditation to use to extend healing or love to a loved one who may be far away. When I and my wife are away from each other we choose a time to meditate together in this way each day, and at other times we will drop in for a visit or just to say, 'I love you.' With practice you will learn to intimately sense and integrate these three dimensions of aliveness within you. As you bring more attention to the dynamic interplay of form-energy-openness in your life, this inner wisdom will become more apparent and will enrich the quality of your relationships as well.

30 *Matrix of mind*

The following meditation can open the way to a direct and profound insight into the nature of mind and perceived phenomena.

Envision a luminous sphere spontaneously and effortlessly appearing in the space before you. Allow its luminous clarity to pervade the surrounding space with a sense of both luminous clarity and 'knowingness.'

Next envision similar spheres of luminous knowingness spontaneously and naturally emerging from the space above and below and to either side of the original sphere, thus forming a cluster of five. Now envision that each of these secondary spheres becomes the center of another cluster of five. Then allow each of these spheres to become a nucleus of further multiples of this five-fold patterning. Continue to multiply these lights out in clusters of four spheres, each of which become a nucleus for a further cluster, until the whole space is pervaded by a unified field of luminous knowingness.

Another approach to this meditation is to envision a sphere of luminous knowingness spontaneously arising at your own center of mindbody. Sense and feel its luminous knowingness pervading the whole space within and around you. Envision in the field of space surrounding you that similar spheres of luminous clarity emerge before you, behind you, to your left and right as well as above and below you. Each of these spheres is identical and all together they form a matrix of seven with six clustered around the central sphere. Beginning with the sphere before you, envision this sphere now becoming the center of a similar cluster with six around it. Then one by one allow each of the primary spheres around you to become the center of a new cluster, a higher order of luminous knowing spheres. Continue to multiply these lights out in clusters of six spheres, each of which become the nucleus for a further cluster, until the whole space within and surrounding you is pervaded by a unified matrix of knowing luminosity.

Bring an effortless and quietly joyful mind to this meditation. Avoid struggling or trying too hard to get it right, but simply practice again and again until it become effortless to multiply these luminous spheres and establish this matrix of mind.

Practice dissolving yourself and the world into this unified clarity. As sights, sounds, colors and other phenomena begin to emerge within and around you, allow each new experience whether sensory or mental to be regarded as a spontaneous, selfless, creative play of mind.

Through this meditation you may come to know mind as intimately pervading and unifying the field of your experience. Within this matrix of mind know that you can loosen your need for an 'I' or 'experiencer' that stands separate from others and from perceived objects. Though appearances may continue to appear distinct and separate from you, gradually the practice of this meditation will reveal that the nature of mind and the world it perceives is actually non-dual and intimately related.

Part Four
More strategies for mental fitness

Fishing baskets are used to catch fish, but when the fish are caught, the men forget the baskets. Snares are used to catch hares, but when the hares are caught, men forget the snares. Words are used to convey ideas, but when the ideas are grasped men forget the words
Chuang Tzu

1 *Strategies for mastering stress*

Life's myriad of changes often lead to an accumulation of stress. Here is a compendium of simple, commonsense strategies for transforming mental and physical tension into energy creatively and effectively expressed. None of these strategies are new. Many will be familiar to you, but we often need to be reminded. Circle the ones you'd like to remember more often. Then add your own to the list:

Take time to be alone on a regular basis, to listen to your heart, check your intentions, re-evaluate your goals and your activites.

Simplify your life! Start eliminating the trivia.

Take deep, slow breaths frequently, especially while on the phone, in the car, or waiting for something or someone. Use any opportunity to relax and revitalize yourself.

Plan to do something each day that gives you energy, something you love to do, something just for you.

When you're concerned about something, talk it over with someone you trust, or write down your feelings.

Say 'No' when asked to do something you really don't want to do. Read a book on assertiveness if you have trouble doing this in a firm but kind way.

Remember to use helpful clichés such as, 'In a hundred years, who will know the difference?' 'What doesn't weaken us, makes us stronger,' or 'Whether you think you can or you think you can't you're right.'

Exercise regularly!

Remember, it takes less energy to get an unpleasant task done right now, than to worry about it all day.

Take time to be with nature, people, music and children. Even in the city, noticing the seasonal changes of the sky or watching people's faces can be a good harmonizer.

Practice consciously doing one thing at a time, keeping your mind focused on the present. Do whatever you're doing more slowly, more intentionally, and with more awareness and respect.

Choose not to waste your precious present life on guilt about the past or concern for the future.

Learn a variety of relaxation techniques and practice at least one regularly.

When you find yourself repeatedly angry in similar situations, ask yourself, 'What can I learn from this?' Anyone or anything that can make you angry is showing you how you yourself let yourself be controlled by expectations of how someone or something should be. When we accept others, ourselves and situations for what they are, we become more effective in influencing them to change in the way that we'd like them to.

Practice basic communication skills such as 'I' statements, paraphrasing and active listening. Change the phrase 'I need' into 'I want,' and 'I have to' into 'I choose to.' Notice the difference when you say 'I choose to' instead of 'I have to.'

Become more aware of the demands you place on yourself, your environment and on others to be different from how they are at any moment. Demands are tremendous sources of stress.

If your schedule is busy, prioritize your activities and do the most important ones first.

When you read your mail, act on it immediately, don't put it off.

Take frequent relaxation breaks.

Carry a card with four or five personal affirmations written on it (for example, I am calm and relaxed. I am confident and capable of handling any situation, etc.)

Organize your life to include time for fun, spontaneity and

open spaces. Set a realistic schedule allowing some transition time between activities. Eliminate unnecessary commitments.

Laugh more.

Learn to delegate responsibility.

Treat yourself to a massage, learn to massage your own neck, shoulders and feet.

Monitor your intake of sugar, salt, caffeine and alcohol.

Create and maintain a personal support system — people with whom you can be 'vulnerable.'

Seek out friends or professional help when you feel unable to cope.

Watch clouds or moving water. Notice the silence between sounds, the space between thoughts.

Remember to stop and smell the flowers.

2 Guidelines for creative visualization

Consciously or unconsciously, we are continually creating mental images: memories, future fantasies, dreams and visions of scenarios that may never happen, daydreams, and our own self-image along with the many projections and expectations we put on others. Indeed, only seldom do we simply experience a moment of perception without attaching to it some kind of associated imagery. By developing skills in creative visualization meditation and mental stimulation, we are learning to understand and take control of this previously unconscious process that has up till now controlled our lives.

In fact, every image we create directly influences our body. Thinking of feeling the warmth of the sun, for example, can trigger a response that dilates the blood vessels and warms the hands. The image of tasting a lemon can cause saliva to flow and our mouths to pucker. Images of aggression can lead to the secretion of hormones associated with anger or fear, increasing our heart rate and muscle tension. Similarly, images of tender caresses can lead to a feeling of sexual arousal, whilst memories of an argument can trigger physical responses leading to a headache or heart palpitation.

Although an actual encounter or experience may only last a minute, we can use our capacity to remember or anticipate the experience in order to recreate the same reaction over and over again. By becoming aware of the images that we create and learning how to control this human faculty, we can not only master psychosomatic symptoms associated with stress, anxiety and worry, but also energize and develop positive qualities of mind.

The following are a variety of techniques for developing your capacity and skills using visualization techniques. Since we all have our own style, these are intended as guidelines only — with practice you will come to understand and develop your own imagery.

1. *Kinesthetic approach*

Visualize an object. Now imagine what it would be like to reach out and *touch* that object. If you are visualizing an apple, say, it may be helpful to actually hold or remember what it felt like to hold an apple. If you are visualizing a person, imagine or recall what it would be like to reach out and touch them. Recall the texture of their hair, skin, the size and contour of their hand and body.

2. *Affirming the image*

Whether or not you can actually see or feel the image, mentally *affirm* that it is indeed there. This is like waking up one morning to find your surroundings shrouded in thick fog, although you cannot actually see the houses and trees around you, you will still know that they are actually there. You should feel the same confidence when generating your images. You can think that the image is actually there in front of you but that your eyes are closed so you can't actually see it directly. If you are imaging an internal feeling, mentally or emotionally affirm that it is indeed happening within you, but at a level of sensitivity below your threshold of awareness.

3. *Imaging is not always visual*

For example, can you imagine hearing the tune 'Jingle Bells?' Is anyone near you singing it...? Likewise, can you imagine the fragrance of a rose...the taste of lemon... the warmth and crackle of a campfire...? Imaging works best when you involve all of your senses to create a multisensory gestalt of holographic experience.

4. *Imaging in three dimensions*

Allow your images to take on a three-dimensional quality rather than appearing flat and two-dimensional. Imagine that you could walk around it, view it from all sides, above and below. Sense its depth, volume, shape and position in space.

5. *Dynamic quality*

Allow your images to take on a living, energetic, resonant, luminous quality. Allow the images to move, flow and change. If portions seem to fade out or dissolve, just gently recreate or bring those parts back into focus.

6. *Fill in the details*

It may be helpful to begin with a sense of the outline of an object and then to fill in the details. For example, when visualizing a person begin by imagining their shape or form and then mentally add the details as clearly as possible. Along the way, previously established aspects may fade. If so, in a very relaxed and effortless manner, bring back the missing details.

7. *Begin with a piece of the image*

Sometimes you may wish to begin with a tiny piece of the image and then mentally build it up from there. For example, you may begin by imagining a person's smile, then mentally adding their face and body.

8. *Affirm the completeness of the image or process*

Imagine that your visualized objects or processes are complete, whole and perfect. Although the total image may not appear to you clearly, affirm its completeness. If, for example, you are visualizing a healing process, imagine that it is worked through to completion. See and feel yourself as healed and whole. Let your mind become accustomed to viewing yourself in this way.

9. *Spontaneous imagery*

As you begin to relax deeply, or in times of extreme stress, vivid images may spontaneously emerge from your own deep consciousness. These images may be holograms of rich personal meaning and value for you. They may be useful in giving you clues for enhancing your healing, creativity, growth and performance. See these images in their dynamic fluid nature. Allow them to move, change and flow. If they do seem to have special meaning for you, use that.

10. *Universal and archetypal images*

At times of deep relaxation or great stress, vivid images may appear to you. These are mental patterns arising from the deep levels of your psyche. These images have been recorded by many cultures and individuals throughout the ages, representing a dynamic and living dimension of primordial and universal wisdom, graphically coded into the genetic matrix and deep psyche of all beings.

11. *Objectless imagery*

Some of the most powerful types of imagery meditations for enhancing health, performance and understanding of the mind involve using imagery of volume, distance and spatial relationships. For example, can you imagine the distance from the top of your head to the ceiling? Is it possible for you to imagine the volume of your body? Can you imagine the space or distance between the buildings in your neighborhood? Used in this way, you can begin to transform your images of yourself and the world in which you live. You become intimately aware of space as a medium that connects everything. It doesn't separate things. The same imagery can be brought to sound and silence. For example, can you imagine noticing the silence before, between and after sounds? How about noticing the space between your thoughts or the images that float through your mind...?

3 Transforming pain

Spacetime view of health and disease tells us that a vital part of the goal of every therapist (educator and spiritual friend) is to help the sick person (and we are all somewhat diseased) towards a reordering of his world view. We must help him to realize that he is a process in spacetime, not an isolated entity who is fragmented from the world of the healthy and adrift in flowing time, moving slowly towards extermination. To the extent that we accomplish this task, we are a healer.

Larry Dossey

Pain and dissatisfaction bring many people onto a path of action, inner growth and personal investigation. There are the sufferings of pain in the body manifesting as injury, disease, hunger, immobility and dying. There are also the sufferings of mental anguish and disease of mind experienced as anxiety and fear, loneliness, confusion, or dissatisfaction which lead many people to look for skills to cope with, if not to master, their discomfort. There is also the suffering of the heart that has closed to itself out of guilt, blame, unworthiness or shame and which has shut off from the world out of anger, jealousy or fear. All of these conditions are painful and unsatisfactory. If our level of awareness is low, it takes more pain to get our attention. If we

learn to pay attention to our minds, bodies and relationships the warning signs of pain will become apparent and
can be dealt with when they are just whispers rather than
waiting for them to become screams.

Once recognized, our suffering may lead us to search for
methods to heal the wounds in our bodies and minds, our
hearts or egos. Some methods distract us or take our attention elsewhere, effectively blocking our awareness of
pain and often allowing conditions to worsen and further
deteriorate. Other methods enable us to better understand
the changing nature of our pain and to live more comfortably with the conditions in our bodies and in our lives that
we associate with our suffering. Still other strategies are
truly effective means of eradicating the causes of our suffering and putting an end to our mental and physical
disease.

Traditionally, different meditation techniques have been
effectively applied to mask, cope with or master pain.
Though concentrative techniques can be effective at mask-
ing the pain, the emphasis of applying meditation to working with pain is that of directly investigating and understanding it. Upon careful examination of the field of sensations that we label as 'pain,' we find that it is not a thing or
unchanging entity. Rather pain is a non-entity, a dynamic
field of sensations and feelings that changes with each
moment and with each state of mind. The courage to face
and understand our own suffering is the first step to working
effectively with our own pain. It is also the first step in
learning to open our hearts and minds enabling us to empathize and compassionately relate to the sufferings of
others. Pain is universally unsatisfactory and by understanding our own wish to be free from our suffering, we
begin to develop greater compassion wishing that others
might be free as well.

Over the years I've worked with thousands of people in
pain. Our unit at the hospital functioned as an unoffical pain
clinic. Time after time I worked with people in intractable

pain due to injury, cancer, nerve damage or fatal illness. From these people I learned that the greatest suffering did not come from the torn or rotting flesh, or the tumor or the bed sores but from their mental interpretation and response to the situation. Fear, helplessness, frustration, anger, guilt and blame were clearly effective methods of intensifying the pain, constricting the body and mind to isolate, contract and cut off that part of oneself from healing. Those who learn to open to pain, to investigate it and to allow it to change, flow and float freely in their bodies, take the first step toward mastering pain. Though this openness does not mean that the pain will go away, it does create a mental and emotional space in which pain is no longer related to as the enemy or as an emergency. With this openness we are able to accept, nurture and love the part of us that is in pain. If we then bring the same quality of openness and reflection to our thoughts and emotional feelings, we will learn to recognize the patterns of mind that intensify our suffering and those patterns of mind that bring greater harmony. In this way we become more responsible for optimizing our own self healing potentials.

A further quantum leap in working with pain comes when we begin to use our own experience of pain as a means of opening the heart in a caring and compassionate way to others. At this stage our self-centered fixation on our own suffering is transformed into a genuinely selfless outpouring of love, compassion and caring which is mentally or even physically offered to others.

As I write this, the image of a man dying with AIDS comes to mind. He was a very spiritual man whose doctor had referred him to me to learn meditation in order to better work with his extreme discomfort and face his impending death. At one of our visits, he described to me how during his sleepless hours through the day and night he would practice the heartfelt extension of love and compassion to others: the dying child down the hall, patients in all the hospitals in the vicinity, his family, and all others who were suffering as he was. Though isolated from most human contact, he found that reaching out to others in a heartfelt and sincere way somehow put his own pain into perspective, and his suffering diminished.

Approached in the right state of mind many of the techiques in this book are effective means for working with physical, emotional and mental pain and for coming to a deeper sense of our own wholeness.

Consciousness is the medium which carries the messages that compose experience. Psychotherapies are concerned with these messages and their meanings; meditation instead directs itself to the nature of the medium, consciousness. These two approaches are by no means mutually exclusive, but rather complementary. A therapy of the future may integrate techniques from both approaches, possibly producing a change in the whole person more thorough-going and more potent than either in isolation.
Daniel Goleman

4 Balancing breath, brain and mind

Place a mirror up to your nose and breath naturally. As you look at the two pools of condensation on the mirror you will notice that one is larger than the other. In fact, if you check throughout the day, you will notice that at any time you are breathing predominantly through one nostril or the other.

Every ninety minutes to two hours the dominant nostril changes and this shift will happen in a matter of minutes. For most people, the shift in dominance goes from right to left and back again roughly ten to twelve times every twenty-four hours. This cycle of naturally alternating breathing cycles has been known to inner science traditions for thousands of years, though it is only in the last decade that modern science has recognized and studied it.

One of the principle reasons for this scientific interest is that breathing cycles appear to mirror shifts in brain function from one hemisphere to the other. The shift in dominant nostrils is directly related to a shift in dominance between the two hemispheres of the brain, as well as a shift in the predominant mode of mental functioning.

Current theories of brain function associate two primary modes of functioning with each of the brain's hemispheres. The left hemisphere is associated with rational, linear, analytic, verbal modes of information processing that bring a high resolution to the details of a situation. The right hemisphere of the brain is associated with more global, intuitive, spatial, non-linear modes of information integration that give a sense of the overlying patterns and gestalt of a situation. Recent studies indicate that the functions of either hemisphere are augmented and enhanced when you are breathing predominantly through either nostril. Not only is there a shift in one's state of mind, but also in the fluctuations of neuro-transmitters and nervous system activity throughout the entire body. (Note, however, that these functions may be reversed if you are left and not right handed.)

Some day this understanding may provide modern science with valuable insight into the mechanisms and treatment of mental disorders. At a practical level, it may provide us with simple yet effective tools for shifting our brain-mind dominance towards the more logical and analytical mode of the left hemisphere or conversely towards the more intuitive or perceptual mode associated with right hemisphere function. Understanding these shifts in brain-mind function may also help you see why you can have an easier time balancing your cheque book, say, while in a right nostril (left hemisphere) phase of dominance, or have more appreciation of an art exhibition or concert while breathing through a left nostril (right hemisphere) dominant cycle.

For thousands of years varieties of techniques have been used to optimize brain function by balancing the subtle energies of the mindbody. According to ancient traditions of meditation, the best time to meditate is when the breath flow is balanced between the two nostrils. This time of balance will occur in two ways: either naturally during the transition time between nostril dominance, when the energies of mind, brain and body are most balanced *or* when the meditator brings about this balance through techniques such as the one described below. In contemporary neurophysical terms, these times of balance would allow for an integration of rational and intuitive, detailed and global functions associated with the two hemispheres of the brain. At these times, information flows more smoothly across the corpus collosum, a bundle of brain fibres that form the communications link between the two sides of the brain.

Understanding the breath-brain functions can not only enhance your meditation but also be used to fine-tune your mindbody throughout the day. To do this, simply bring your attention to your breath flow, nostril dominance and predominant mode of mind frequently. If you find it difficult to accomplish a particular task with your present state of mind-brain, try shifting your breathing pattern to the other hemisphere and mind-style. To do this, first identify which nostril you are breathing through. Then, inhale through the new nostril, exhaling through the previously predominant one, for a few minutes until the breathing feels like it has shifted. This can be enhanced by visualizing the breath flow as clearing the nostrils and energizing the functions of the opposite brain hemisphere.

It is especially useful to apply these techniques:

1. If you notice that your mind is dull, diffuse or day-dreamy when you need to accomplish a task requiring detailed precise attention.

2. If you feel swept away by disruptive emotional feelings or confusion.

3. Since studies show that appetite and digestion are enhanced while we are in a right nostril dominant breathing cycle, you may chose to eat at times when this pattern occurs naturally, or even consciously shift this balance if you need to eat at another time.

4. Similarly, most people will find that deep sleep is more quickly and easily achieved by laying on the right side, which shifts the breath dominance to the left nostril.

5 *Sports: a Western yoga*

Sports, music and dance are perhaps the closest disciplines to meditative training that most Westerners know. Each of these activities demands that we be fully present in what we are doing, yet at the same time maintain a suppleness and flow with the moment to moment changes of the process. The mental and physical discipline of sports or the performing arts trains the mind to access a wide range of concentrative and meditative states. The exhilaration of these activities is not just due to physical demands but is also related to the naturally blissful, energized, creative and peaceful experience of the quiet and concentrated mind.

Once we have successfully harnessed our wandering thoughts, new dimensions of awareness open up. Momentary peak experiences of being in the 'flow state' with its effortless and extraordinary performance are quite common to athletes and artists. These moments of grace seem to happen spontaneously and are seldom understood or replicable, yet their memory lingers...and our standards for what we *know* is possible may never be the same again.

The numerous examples of flow state or peak performance experiences reported by athletes and sports teams — though described by 'jocks' rather than bearded sages — are strikingly similar to classical concentrative and meditative experiences.

Certainly not all of us have to dedicate our life to our sport, rather we can dedicate our sport to our life — approaching our training as a vehicle for honing those human qualities that enhance virtually all of the endeavors we set our minds to. There are countless men and women who have discovered or learned how to calm their minds through breath control, to transmute anger and fear into power, to let go as well as to hold on, to be sensitive and caring rather than callous. By learning to blend with inner and outer natural laws many athletes have been able to tap reservoirs of extraordinary power, skill, and understanding, allowing them to perform in remarkable ways.

Sports training through its physical actions, activates those human sources that develop an athletes personality, improve physical and psychological skills, and discover unlimited possibilities of the human mind and body. Performance is only a means to facilitate the athlete's self-actualization, to help athletes create in hard work undisputable cultural values of modern humanity.
Tadeuz Rychta,
Polish sports psychologist

The arena of athletic competition provides a laboratory in which mindbody skills can be tested and refined. Though the motivation may be different, the commitment and rigorous discipline of modern athletes is closely akin to practitioners of inner contemplative traditions. When faced with an equal in competition, one is forced to draw upon resources that are ordinarily considered to be beyond the range of one's capabilities. The orchestration of mental factors necessary to reach for this domain of extraordinary performance has catapulted many individuals and teams into realms of experience that are ordinarily the territory of yogis, mystics, and contemplatives.

The recent trend in physical fitness has raised and deepened the awareness of many people. This has resulted in a second wave of interest that incorporates the conscious cultivation of mental fitness skills in conjunction with the practice of athletic and martial arts disciplines. On the field or on the mat, one receives moment to moment feedback on the interrelationship of mind and body. With practice one learns to minimize those mental and physical states that decrease and impair one's effectiveness, and to increase those that enhance one's performance.

Let us look at some examples of how these extraordinary states of mind can be developed and expressed in the arena of our life.

The dynamic state of personal excellence in action has been studied in contemporary psychology by Czikzent-minalyi, who has studied a broad range of intrinsically rewarding activities, all of which are marked by a similar experience, that he calls 'the flow.' The key elements of the flow are:

1. The merging of action and awareness in sustained, non-distractable concentration on the task at hand.
2. The focusing of attention on a limited field of stimuli.
3. Self-forgetfulness with heightened awareness of function and body states related to the involving activity.
4. Skills adequate to meet the environmental demand.
5. Clarity regarding situation cues and appropriate responses.

Flow states arise when there is an optimal correspondance between one's capability and the demands of the moment. The spectrum of the flow experience is bordered on the one hand by anxiety inducing situations where demands exceed one's capability and on the other by boredom where one's capability far exceeds the demand.

A person in flow operates from a unified perspective. Their attention is completely absorbed into the activity without any dualistic sense of an 'I' who is doing something. The moment this awareness is split and one becomes self-conscious, the flow state is interrupted.

A neurophysical interpretation of the significant characteristics of the flow state reveals that it requires both precision and fluidity in neurologic patterning, so that the brain can change in dynamic response to the fluctuating situational requirements. The flow state is not a static pattern of ongoing arousal, rather it demands flexibility. The chronically anxious or habitually aroused individual is likely to confront more situations where their internal state is inappropriately tuned to environmental demands and thus unable to access a flow state. Changing circumstances require changing internal states.

There are two ways of increasing the likelihood of flow experience: regulating environmental challenge to fit one's skills, as in games, or self-regulation of internal capacities to meet a greater variation in external demands. The disadvantage of the first is that flow remains situation bound, relying on a given set of environmental cues for its elicitation. Mental fitness disciplines such as relaxation, concentration, meditation, biofeedback, hemisynchronous brain states, and martial arts would fulfil the latter strategy of producing a shift in internal state. Learning such skills maximizes the possibility for us to enter the flow state, while lessening the need to control the environment. Moreover, these approaches teach how to use a variety of self-tuning technologies that alter the basic process of mind, so that situations can be met from a flow state more frequently.

Epstein has recently suggested that one of the most rewarding aspects of long distance running is what some have called the runner's high. She described it as 'drifting' ...formerly known as 'dreaming your life away.' Epstein states:

> *The standard by which I measure my run is not*
> *the degree to which I sweat or how fast a pace I set.*
> *It is not important to me whether I beat my own*
> *record or surpass my friends. Just give me a quiet,*
> *pleasant area to run and let me drift.*

Epstein also noted that the evaluation of her runs was based on the amount of drifting she had been able to accomplish. It was acceptable occasionally to focus on some unusual or interesting sight, but speedy return to the state of drift was paramount.

One of the most celebrated descriptions of an experiential immersion in flow was given by ex-San Francisco quarterback John Brodie. In an interview with Michael Murphy, founder of Esalen Institute, Brodie described this extraordinary way of perceiving space and time:

Often in the heat and excitement of a game, a player's perception and coordination will improve dramatically. At times, and with increasing frequency now, I experience a kind of clarity that I've never seen adequately described in a football story. Sometimes, for example, time seems to slow way down in an uncanny way, as if everyone were moving in slow motion. It seems as if I have all the time in the world to watch the receivers run their patterns, and yet I know the defensive line is coming at me just as fast as ever. I know perfectly well how hard and fast those guys are coming and yet the whole thing seems like a movie or a dance in slow motion. It's beautiful.

Descriptions by athletes of such events are abundant. These are common and are not purely the exclusive domain of the professional athlete. The time-defying total absorption of the backyard athlete or the runner's high of the professional marathon may be similar in origin. These experiences suggest that an alternative to the ordinary means of experiencing space and time lies within us all. Our challenge is to understand the mechanisms of these experiences and help people learn to consciously evoke these states rather than unconsciously stumble into them.

Lester Fehmi describes this state as 'an unobstructed flowing of energy and experience through the mindbody system.' He designed a method he called 'open focus training' that works with spatial awareness and objectless imagery to decrease ordinary self-consciousness and the awareness of time and space. This state of integration he calls 'no-time.' He concludes that the way we attend affects all waking activity. Research on open focus and similar meditation techniques confirms that the disposition of attention, more than any other process of behavior that one can learn to control directly governs one's state of mental and physiological well-being.

Explanation of the synchronous entrainment of a team is usually nebulous and vague. Yet theologian Michael Novak suggests that precise and coherent reorganization of individual and team resonance is demonstrated by these moments of team excellence.

> *When a collection of individuals first jells as a team, and truly begins to react as a five-headed or eleven-headed unit rather than as an aggregate of five or eleven individuals, you can almost hear the click; a new kind of reality comes into existence at a new level of human development. A basketball team, for example, can click into and out of this reality many times during the same game; and each player, as well as the coach and the fans can detect the difference . . .for those who have participated in a team that has known the click of camaraderie, the experience is unforgettable, like that of having attained, for a while at least, a higher level of existence; existence as it ought to be.*

With diligent practice and unwavering commitment, these extraordinary states of personal and team excellence can become the norm and not the fleeting exception. In an article entitled 'The Liberal Arts and the Martial Arts' that appeared in the New York Times, Donald Levine described the stages of development that lead to the pinnacles of performance.

> *One begins by self-consciously practicing a certain technique. One proceeds slowly, deliberately, reflectively; but one keeps on practicing until the technique becomes internalized and one is no longer self-conscious when executing it. After a set of techniques has been thoroughly internalized, one begins to grasp the principles behind them. And finally, when one has understood and internalized the basic principles, one no longer responds mechanically to a given attack, but begins to use the art creatively and in a manner whereby one's individual style and insights can find expression.*

The fast-paced, colorful and demanding nature of sports initially captures the interest of many people interested in testing the potential of their mind and body. With continued training, many athletes learn to equally value training time in the quiet depths of the mind as a domain of free play, self-healing and regeneration, and as a source of strength and power to access new dimensions of performance. The continued melding of mental and physical technologies will empower athletes and teams of the future with the skills to far surpass the performance norms of today. With this contemporary approach to mental fitness training the best of both modern and ancient disciplines will be blended enabling us to continually expand our understanding of what is possible for a human being or a team to accomplish.

6 Biofeedback: technology of mindbody and spirit

Each of us possesses everything that is necessary to explore our deepest nature . . . No one else in all human kind can do it for us. The responsibility and opportunity for becoming aware of all that we most truly are and sharing it with others is ultimately our own.

Roger Walsh and Dean Shapiro

Life is learning, and all learning depends on feedback. If we play an instrument, we listen to the quality of music and change the tuning accordingly. If we are cooking, we adjust the flavor of the food by tasting it, if we are doing target practice we adjust our aim by watching the result of our shots. When skiing or surfing we continually rely upon feedback to refine our skills and reach our goals, and the same is true with regards living and working in relationships. By attending to the feedback of our bodies, friends and environment we can learn, grow and become more successful and effective in our lives.

Advances in modern medical technology are now making it possible to tune into the subtle changes of our own body by measuring, amplifying and displaying this information for us to see. This fedback information about one's own biology is called biofeedback.

The human body is extremely responsive to mental imagery and intentions. The epidemic of stress related illnesses and breakthroughs in human performance represent two ends of the spectrum of mental influence on our physical condition. We each were born with the capacity to enhance or undermine the quality of our health, yet most of us have never learned the basic skills for promoting our own health and well-being.

To demonstrate the potential for mental control of physiological systems, researchers Elmer and Alice Green of the Menninger Foundation invited an accomplished yogi, Swami Rama, to their psychophysiological control laboratory. The Swami was wired to two temperature sensors so as to measure the change of blood flow to different parts of the palm of his hand. Under rigorous experimental conditions the researchers watched as the Swami demonstrated his ability to perform a medical miracle by consciously altering his circulation to make one part of his palm nearly seventeen degrees warmer than an area a couple of inches away. A university student who had heard about the experiment decided to see if he could learn the same control using thermal biofeedback. Within two weeks he had achieved the same degree of extraordinary physiological control that the yogi admitted had taken him years to learn. (For more information see *Beyond Biofeedback* by Alyce and Elmer Green.)

Imagine the implications for modern medicine and science if many people were to learn to control, self regulate and optimize their own body functions. Imagine what it would mean if the millions of people who needlessly suffer from stress related illnesses were to learn the skills to consciously relax their tense muscles, and reduce the symptoms of uptightness that they have stored in their digestive, circulatory, respiratory and nervous systems.

Biofeedback provides us with tools to accelerate our learning of mindbody fine-tuning. The key to this learning is assuming greater responsibility for our own health. As mentioned earlier, there are two strategies for recognizing disease. One is to allow the warning signs of imbalance to accumulate to the point of extreme discomfort or debilitation, and then attempt to intercede with some radical or drastic intervention.

The alternative is to refine and intensify our internal awareness in order to recognize the initial warning signs of disease and then to apply a simple remedy.

Modern biofeedback technology is now enabling us to monitor and amplify many subtle signals from our bodies in order to bring information about ordinarily unnoticed and unconscious physiological processes to the level of conscious awareness. This revolution in modern science and medicine is a reversal of our use of familiar technology. In many cases similar or simplified versions of equipment that health care professionals have tested and measured us with is now being used to enable us to directly receive on line biological information about our own body. Instead of someone else interpreting the monitor readings and then treating us, we can gain greater self-awareness of our internal process. In this way, we can experiment to find the subtle internal movement of mind that changes our body in the desired manner.

Every change in the physiological state is accompanied by an appropriate change in the mental-emotional state, conscious or unconscious; and conversely, every change in the mental-emotional state, conscious or unconscious, is accompanied by an appropriate change in the physiological state . . .
Alyce and Elmer Green

Any method that helps us to amplify the previously unconscious interplay of mental, emotional and physiological processes, enables us to learn how to change our lives for the better.

In practice it is almost as simple to use biofeedback to find out about our inner state of body as it is to use a mirror to find out about our outer appearance. What happens is that a passive sensor is attached over a site of muscle tension, blood flow, brain waves or other physiological signal. The signal is then amplified and fedback to the person whose body it is coming from. Changes in the physiological state modulate the feedback signal that may be in the form of a tone that changes in frequency or loudness, a light bar or graph, a digital score, or computor game. For example, if we were using a biofeedback machine called an EMG (Electromyograph), we would place a sensor over a tight muscle in a muscular region that is frequently tense. We would then use a monitor to amplify and feedback information about subtle increases and decreases of tension in order to quickly learn how to recognize and control the level of our tension or relaxation. In a similar way, one can learn to control hypertension, circulation, stress responses, improve one's eyesight or enhance one's state of brain and mind.

Contrary to most medical treatments, with biofeedback training *you are the one in control*. With practice, most people quickly learn how to change their internal state for the better. Given the choice of energizing old harmful and self-abusive habits or not, a person learns an empowered option to go for the good.

Biofeedback involves the development of three primary qualities of mind: attention, intention and imagery.

Attention is the quality of mind that knows what we are attending to. To the degree that we can keep our attention on what we are doing; we can say that our attention is concentrated and stable.

Intention is the capacity that enables us to mentally direct our attention and action towards accomplishing our goals.

Imagery is the primary control language that enables us to communicate with our own bodies. Intention energizes and helps manifest our mental imagery of what is possible.

The misalignment of these factors allows our subconscious fears and anxieties to become physically manifest as disease, debilitation, or a vulnerability to accidents. Properly orchestrated and consciously directed, the power of our attention, intention and imagery synergize to enable us to realize our capacity for extraordinary levels of health and performance.

I've been asked if biofeedback is 'electronic Zen'? Well, the machines cannot do the learning for you, but they can help you accelerate your learning to distinguish the mental states and attitudes that lead you toward or away from the physiological states of health or peak performance. One day I was showing Chagdud Rinpoche, a respected Tibetan doctor and accomplished meditator, how thermal biofeedback training worked when he exclaimed: 'Ah! When I try to meditate it does not work. When I meditate it works!'

Regardless of the discipline, whether relaxation, concentration, meditation or biofeedback, maximizing effort does not optimize our control. In fact, the state of mind most successful in directing our body to change for the better is referred to as 'passive volition,' 'voluntary surrender' or 'doing without trying.' This state of mind is best tuned into by having a clear intention and image of the desired state of mindbody and then simply allowing it to happen effortlessly. Your success in the biofeedback process itself will let you know when you are on the right track and when you are trying too hard.

A contemporary revolution in health care is finding thousands of people actively involved in learning to control the diseases of modern times including hypertension, tension, migraine headaches, circulatory disorders, gastrointestinal disorders, chronic muscle tension, bruxism and TMJ pain, chronic anxiety, compulsive addictions, and other stress related symptoms with psychophysical self-regulation training including meditation and biofeedback. As health care costs continue to climb, the practical sense and applications of biofeedback, and the skills described in this book will grow in value.

Peak performance applications of biofeedback have attracted the attention of many of the world's finest athletes, performing artists and creative minds who are interested in learning to reduce inefficient physical and mental patterns in order to train their bodies and brains for optimal performance. In pursuit of excellence athletes, elite troups and corporate executives are now spending more time mentally rehearsing and refining their skills through the internal arts of meditation, visualization and biofeedback assisted fine tuning.

Biofeedback is frequently used for teaching pain control and relaxation skills, enhancing neuromuscular coordination, speeding recovery time from illness, strokes, injury and disease. Advanced applications of biofeedback training are helping people to increase the speed and accuracy of their senses, to accelerate their learning and to turn on states of brain associated with mental calm, clarity and creativity.

Most importantly, biofeedback is a tool for increasing our self awareness and confidence in accepting greater responsibility to contribute to our own disease or well-being. Properly trained to interpret the myriad of subtle messages our bodies are sending us it is less likely that we will ignore the blatant warning whispers of accumulating stress and tension that unheeded may lead to the life threatening diseases.

We are rapidly moving towards the day when many people will understand their bodies. In the near future, revolutions in education will prioritize biofeedback and self regulation training as a fourth 'R' in grade schools, encouraging a new generation of children to grow up with an attitude of self empowerment and responsibility for their own disease and well-being. As the stresses of our modern world continue to accelerate, adult interest in biofeedback could find many people learning to master their own stress and enhance their performance. Instead of watching TV, evenings could be spent in digitally enhanced contemplations assisted by computor graphics biofeedback games. Creativity and microcircuitry and currently being combined to build a future generation of video arcades in which the winners will be the ones with the greatest psychophysical knowledge. Biofeedback games could introduce us to new modes of competition and cooperation where winning is determined by whoever can relax the most or where the goal becomes to quickly synchronize one's heart beats or brain waves with one's challenger.

Within the next decade we will likely witness a revolution in technology and research in human consciousness, coinciding with the refinement of microcircuitry and so on. As electronic circuitry becomes more and more sensitive to subtle changes in electromagnetic fields, the quantum effects of the mind on matter will become startlingly apparent. Though our minds are continually affecting our physiological state, the immediacy of this affect was only widely known by practitioners of mental training prior to the advent of biofeedback and medical monitoring technology. As we continue to refine our technology and our attention, we will surely discover what inner scientists and meditators have known through direct intuitive experience for millenia — that matter, be it a body or a world, is intimately pervaded by and responsive to the mind.

Research at the Engineering Anomolies Research Project in the School of Engineering at Princeton University, Stanford University and numerous other prestigious institutes worldwide have already begun to investigate and document the impact of conscious focussed intention on altering computer function, bending laser beams and case hardened steel, materializing and dematerializing objects, observing situations beyond the range of ordinary sense perceptions and other paranormal occurences. Even ordinary, untrained people seem to have the latent ability to exercise extraordinary mental abilities challenging many of our cherished assumptions regarding the nature of mind and reality. This trend in research has blown open dimensions of scientific enquiry that will require researchers skilled in both the inner and outer sciences.

Regarding the relationship between extraordinary events, the nature of the mind and biofeedback, one of the great pioneer biofeedback researchers, Barbara Brown, has said:

> *The characteristic and most exasperating aspect of psychic phenomena is unpredictability, which incites the scepticism of many scientists. Yet science knows relatively little about the normal mind function. If we know so little about what is normal, how can we know whether, the paranormal is paranormal or normal?*
>
> *The probability is high that psychic events are predictable. We simply have not found some aspects of psychic phenomena upon which predictability can be based.*
>
> *If mental activity truly originates from our brain cells, then it is logical to assume that psychic phenomena also use these same brain cells. We assume this because psychic activity involves a change in mental activity; otherwise, it could not be integrated, stored, recalled and communicated by human means. Telepathic information must have entry into the universe of the brain cells where the 'picture' of the information is developed. Even if the psychic information gets into the brain supernaturally, it must go through the ordinary channels of brain processing to get out of the brain to be communicated to other people.*
>
> *This means that there is a brain physiological impression of the psychic experience. If that impression is there, then we should be able to find it. If biofeedback can be used with this brain indicator to bring psychic abilities under voluntary predictable control, this will be one of the most explosive discoveries that biofeedback can make.*

Breakthroughs in technology will herald a renaissance of research into the nature of human consciousness as we witness the undeniable effect that mental intention can have on microtechnology — technology that is at the heart of the greatest sources of creative and destructive power in our world. Since these tools are subject to the power of our individual and collective intention even now, surely we will recognize even more to be at stake in the future.

As research into the nature of human creativity, health and peak performance provides us with a clearer image of what is possible for a human being, biofeedback will provide us with a powerful, effective and entertaining means for strengthening those psychophysical latencies within us that will open new dimensions of health, creativity, love, understanding, extraordinary performance and appreciation for the preciousness and potentials of our lives.

*When you practice these precious
teachings, slowly the clouds of
sorrow melt away. And the sun of
wisdom and true joy will be shining
in the clear sky of your mind.*
Kalu Rinpoche

Appendix 1
Summary of Contemporary Meditation Research

*The Association strongly recommends that research
be undertaken in the form of well-controlled studies to
evaluate the specific usefulness, indications,
contraindications, and dangers of meditative
techniques. The research should compare the various
forms of meditation with one another and
with psychotherapeutic and psychopharmacologic
modalities.*
American Psychiatric Association
(position statement on meditation) 1977

PHYSIOLOGICAL EFFECTS	NUMBER OF STUDIES		
	Confirming	*Not confirming*	*Total*
Cardiovascular			
Decreased heart rate	21	10	31
Redistributed blood flow	8	–	8
Decreased blood pressure	21	6	27
Cortical			
Increased alpha	34	–	34
Theta bursts	21	–	21
Beta bursts	10	–	10
Hemisphere synchronization	25	–	25

PHYSIOLOGICAL EFFECTS	NUMBER OF STUDIES		
	Confirming	*Not confirming*	*Total*
Cortical (cont)			
Dehabituation	17	3	20
Specific cortical control	11	—	11
Blood Chemistry			
Decreased adrenal hormones	7	7	14
Increased amino acid/ phenylalanine	1	—	1
Increased prolactin	1	—	1
Decreased growth hormone	1	—	1
Decreased lactates	10	2	12
Increased serotonin	1	—	1
Decreased white blood cell	1	—	1
Decreased red blood cell metabolism	2	—	2
Decreased cholesterol	2	—	2
Metabolism			
Decreased oxygen consumption	43	—	43
Muscular tension			
Decreased muscular tension—EMG	15	—	15
Skin resistence			
Increased skin resistence— GSR	24	9	33
Other			
Salivary changes	11	—	11
Assists in treatment of cancer	14	—	14
Changed body temperature	1	—	1
Alleviation of pain	12	—	12
Enhancement of body control	17	—	17

BEHAVIORAL EFFECTS	NUMBER OF STUDIES		
	Confirming	*Not confirming*	*Total*
Enhanced visual/auditory percept	27	–	27
Faster reaction time	8	3	11
Increased field independence	8	1	9
Improved concentration	11	3	14
Improved intelligence	11	2	13
Roschach shifts	3	–	3
Greater empathy	18	–	18
Regression in service of ego	7	–	7
Increased creativity	7	5	12
Greater self-actualization	20	2	22
Increased hypnotic suggestibility	4	3	7
Less anxiety	17	13	30
Assists psychotherapy	33	2	35
Lessens chemical addiction	12	5	17
SUBJECTIVE REPORTS			
Equanimity	11	–	11
Detachment	6	–	6
Bliss	4	–	4
Energy	7	–	7
Altered body image	8	–	8
Hallucinations	10	–	10

Excerpt from *Contemporary Meditation Research: A Summary of the Field with a Bibliography of 926 Entrees* – by Michel Murphy and Steven Donovan, The Esalen Transformation Project, San Francisco, California, 1985.

Suggested further reading

RELAXATION

Herbert Benson, *The Relaxation Response*, (London: Collins, 1976).

——*Beyond the Relaxation Response*, (New York: Time Books, 1984).

Lester Fehmi and George Fritz, *Open Focus Handbook*, (Princeton: Biofeedback Computers, 1982).

Daniel Goleman, et al. *The Relaxed Body*, (New York: Double. day, 1986).

Tarthang Tulku, *Kum Nye Relaxation:* Vols. 1 & 2, (Berkeley: Dharma Publications, 1978).

CONCENTRATION

Henepola Gunaratana, *The Path of Serenity and Insight*, (Columbia, Missouri: South Asia Books, 1985).

Thich Nhat Hanh, *A Guide to Walking Meditation*, (Berkeley: Paralax, 1985).

Charles Johnston, *The Yoga Sutras of Patanjali*, (London: Watkins, 1974).

Lati Rinbochay, Denma Locho Rinbochay, Leah Zahler, Jeffrey Hopkins, *Meditative States In Tibetan Buddhism*, (London: Wisdom Publications, 1983).

I.K. Taimni, *The Science of Yoga*, (Wheaton: Theosophical Publishing House, A Quest Book, 1961).

Swami Vivekananda, *Raja Yoga*, (New York: Ramakrishna-Vivekananda Center, 1973).

MEDITATION

Basic

Ram Dass, *Journey of Awakening*, (New York: Bantam, 1978).

Anthony Fernand, *Buddhism Made Plain: An Introduction for Christians and Jews*, (Maryknoll: Orbis Books, 1985).

R.M. French, (trans.), *The Way of the Pilgrim*, (New York: Seabury Press, 1977).

Joseph Goldstein, *The Experience of Insight*, (Boston: Shambhala, 1983).

Sonam Gyatso (The Third Dalai Lama), commentary by Tenzin Gyatso (The Fourteeth Dalai Lama), *Essence of Refined Gold*, Glenn H. Mullin, (trans.), (New York: Snow Lion, 1982).

Tenzin Gyatso the Dalai Lama, translated and edited by Jeffrey Hopkins. *Kindness, Clarity and Insight*, (New York: Snow Lion, 1985).

Thich Nhat Hanh, *Miracle of Mindfulness!* (Berkeley: Paralax, 1984).

Stephen Levine, *A Gradual Awakening*, (New York: Doubleday, 1978).

—— *Who Dies? An Investigation of Conscious Living and Conscious Dying*, (New York: Doubleday, 1982).

Kathleen McDonald, *How to Meditate*, (London: Wisdom Publications, 1985).

Anthony de Mello, *Sadhana: A Way to God, Christian Exercises in Eastern Form*, (New York: Doubleday, 1984).

Geshe Rabten, *The Graduated Path to Liberation*, (Delhi: Mahayana Publications, 1983).

—— & Geshe Dhargyey, *Advice From a Spiritual Friend*, (London: Wisdom Publications, 1986).

Deborah Rozman, *Meditating with Children*, (Boulder Creek: University of the Trees Press, 1977).

Reb Zalman Schachter-Shalomi, *The First Step, A Guide for the New Jewish Spirit*, (New York: Bantam Books, 1983).

Shunryu Suzuki, *Zen Mind, Beginner's Mind* (New York: Weatherhill, 1986).

Sujata, *Beginning to See,* (San Francisco: Apple Pie Books, 1985).

Tarthang Tulku, *Gesture of Balance,* (Berkeley: Dharma Publications, 1977).

——*Skillful Means,* (Berkeley: Dharma Publications, 1978).

Thubten Yeshe, *Silent Mind, Holy Mind,* (London: Wisdom Publications, 1978).

—— *Introduction to Tantra,* (London: Wisdom Publications, 1987).

——& Zopa Rinpoche, *Wisdom Energy,* (London: Wisdom Publications, 1984).

Chogyam Trungpa, *Cutting Through Spiritual Materialism,* (Berkeley: Shambhala, 1973).

Geshe Wangchen, *Awakening the Mind of Enlightenment,* (London: Wisdom Publications, 1987).

Intermediate

John Blofeld, *The Zen Teachings of Huang Po* (New York: Grove, 1959).

Garma C.C. Chang, (trans.), *The Hundred Thousand Songs of Milarepa,* Vols. 1 & 2, (Boulder & London: Shambhala, 1977).

Ram Dass, *Grist for the Mill,* (Santa Cruz: Unity Press, 1977).

Anthony de Mello, *The Song of the Bird,* (New York: Doubleday, 1984).

Fred Eppsteiner, Dennis Maloney, (eds.), *The Path of Compassion, Contemporary Writings on Engaged Buddhism,* (Buffalo, N.Y.: Buddhist Peace Fellowship, White Pine Press, 1985).

Daniel Goleman, *Varieties of Meditative Experience,* (New York: Dutton, 1977).

Geshe Kelsang Gyatso, *Meaningful to Behold,* (London: Tharpa, 1986).

—— *Heart of Wisdom,* (London: Tharpa, 1986).

Tenzin Gyatso the Dalai Lama, *Opening the Eye of New Awareness,* (London: Wisdom Publications, 1985).

Kathleen Healy, *Entering the Cave of the Heart: Eastern Ways of Prayer for Western Christians*, (New York: Paulist Press, 1986).

Robert Harry Hover, *How to Direct the Life Force to Dispel Mild Aches and Pains*, (La Mirada, Calif.: 1979).

Kalu Rinpoche, *The Gem Ornament of Manifold Oral Instructions which Benefits Each and Everyone Appropriately*, (San Francisco, KDK Publications, 1986).

—— *The Dharma that Illuminates All Beings Impartially Like the Light of the Sun and the Moon*, (Albany: SUNY, 1986).

Aryeh Kaplan, *Jewish Meditation: A Practical Guide*, (Cambridge: Schoken, 1985).

Pir Vilayat Inayat Khan, *Toward the One*, (London: Harper & Row, 1974).

Jack Kornfield, *Living Buddhist Masters*, (Santa Cruz: Unity Press, 1977).

Lao Tzu, D.C. Lau, *Tao Te Ching*, (Great Britain: Penguin Books, 1963).

Jigme Lingpa, Tulku Thondup (trans.), edited by Brian Beresford, *The Dzogchen, Preliminary Practice of the Innermost Essence*, (Dharamsala, India: Library of Tibetan Works and Archives, 1982).

Brother Lawrence, *Practice of the Presence of God*, (Mount Vernon: Peter Pauper Press, 1967).

Thomas Merton, *Contemplation in a World of Action*, (New York: Doubleday, 1973).

—— *New Seeds of Contemplation* (New York: New Directions, 1976).

Namkhai Norbu, *The Crystal and the Way of Light: Sutra, Tantra, and Dzogchen*, (New York & London: Routledge & Kegan Paul, 1986).

Geshe Rabten, *The Essential Nectar*, (London: Wisdom Publications, 1984).

Paul Reps, *Zen Flesh, Zen Bones*, (Garden City: Doubleday, 1957).

Mike Samuels and Nancy Samuels, *Seeing with the Mind's*

Eye, (New York & Berkeley: Random House/Bookworks, 1975).

Idries Shah, *The Way of the Sufi,* (New York: Dutton, 1970).

Shantideva, Stephen Batchelor (trans.), *A Guide to the Bodhisattva's Way of Life,* (Dharamsala, India: Library of Tibetan Works and Archives, 1979).

Chogyam Trungpa, *Shambhala: the Sacred Path of the Warrior,* (Boston: Shambhala, 1984).

Tarthang Tulku, *Space, Time & Knowledge,* (Berkeley: Dharma Publications, 1977).

—— *Knowledge of Freedom,* (Berkeley: Dharma Publications, 1984).

Advanced

Garma C.C. Chang, *Six Yogas of Naropa and Teachings on Mahamudra,* (New York: Snow Lion, 1986).

Chang Chen Chi (trans.), C.A. Muses, *Esoteric Teachings of the Tibetan Tantra,* (Maine: Samuel Weiser, 1982).

Lama Anagarika Govinda, *Foundations of Tibetan Mysticism,* (New York: Samuel Weiser, 1969).

—— *The Psychological Attitude of Early Buddhist Philosophy,* (New York: Samuel Weiser, 1974).

—— *Creative Meditation and Multi-Dimensional Consciousness,* (Wheaton: The Theosophical Publishing House, 1976).

—— *Psycho-Cosmic Symbolism of the Buddhist Stupa,* (Berkeley: Dharma Publishing, 1976).

Jeffrey Hopkins, *Meditation on Emptiness,* (London: Wisdom Publications, 1983).

Lati Rinbochay and Jeffrey Hopkins, *Death, Intermediate State and Rebirth in Tibetan Buddhism,* (New York: Snow Lion, 1979).

Franklin Merrell-Wolff, *Philosophy of Consciousness Without an Object,* (New York: Julian Press, 1973).

Namkhai Norbu & John M. Reynolds, *The Cycle of Day and Night, A Basic Text on the Practice of Dzog Chen,* (Berkeley: Zhang Zhung Editions, 1984).

BIOGRAPHIES

Tsultrim Allione, *Women of Wisdom*, (London: Arkana, 1986).
J.G. Bennet, *Long Pilgrimage: The Life and Teachings of Shiva-puri Baba*, (San Rafael: Dawn Horse, 1984).
Keith Dowman, *Masters of Mahamudra*, (Albany: SUNY, 1985).
Lama Anagarika Govinda, *The Way of the White Clouds*, (Boston, Shambhala, 1970).
Kalu Rinpoche, *The Chariot for Travelling the Path to Freedom: The Life Story of Kalu Rinpoche*, Kenneth McLeod (trans.) (San Francisco: Kagyu Dharma, 1985).
Jonathan Landaw & Janet Brooke; *Prince Siddhartha*, (London: Wisdom Publications, 1984).
Lobsang Lhalungpa, *The Life of Milarepa*, (Boston: Shambhala, 1984).
Franklin Merrell-Wolff, *Pathways Through Space*, (New York: Julian Press, 1973).
Bernadette Roberts, *The Experience of No-Self*, (Boston: Shambhala: 1984).
—— *The Path to No-Self: Life at the Center*, (Boston: Shambhala: 1985).
B. Alan Wallace, *The Life and Teachings of Geshe Rabten*, (London: Wisdom Publications, forthcoming 1988).
Paramahansa Yogananda, *Autobiography of a Yogi*, (L.A.: SRF, 1985).

SPORTS, PEAK PERFORMANCE AND MARTIAL ARTS

Horst Abrahams, *Skiing Right*, (New York: Harper & Row, 1984).
Charles Garfield, *Peak Performance Strategies & Insights of Americas Most Productive People*, (New York: Morrow, 1986).
—— & Hal Bennett, *Peak Performance: Mental Training Techniques of the World's Greatest Athletes*, (L.A.: Tarcher, 1984).

Richard Strozzi-Heckler, *Aikido and the New Warrior*, (Berkeley: North Atlantic Books, 1985).

Dan Millman, *The Warrior Athlete: Body Mind & Spirit*, (Walpole: Stillpoint, 1985).

Michael Murphy, *Golf in the Kingdom*, (New York: Dell, 1972).

Michael Murphy and Rhea White, *The Psychic Side of Sports*, (London: Addison-Wesley, 1978).

Kay Porter & Judy Foster, *The Mental Athlete: Inner Training for Peak Performance* (L.A.: Wm. C. Brown, 1985).

MEDITATION RESEARCH, PSYCHOTHERAPY AND BIOFEEDBACK

Guy Claxton, (ed.), *Beyond Therapy*, (London: Wisdom Publications, 1986).

Barbara Brown, *New Mind New Body: Biofeedback — New Directions for Mind*, (New York: Harper & Row, 1974).

Alyce and Elmer Green, *Beyond Biofeedback*, (New York: Delecorte, 1977).

Joel Levey, *Meditation as Self Regulation: Practical Applications & Intriguing Implications for Clinicians and Educators*, (Seattle: SportsMind, 1986).

Michael Murphy and Steven Donovan, *Contemporary Meditation Research: A Summary of the Field with a Bibliography of 962 Entrees*, (San Fransisco: Eselen Foundation, 1985).

Claudio Naranjo and Robert Ornstein, *On the Psychology of Meditation*, (New York: Viking, 1971).

Erik Peper, et al. *Mind/Body Integration: Essential Readings in Biofeedback*, (New York: Plenum, 1979).

Deanne H. Shapiro, Jr., *Meditation: Self Regulation Strategy and Altered State of Consciousness*, (Chicago: Aldine, 1980).

—— and Roger Walsh, (eds.), *Meditation: Classic and Contemporary Perspectives*, (Chicago: Aldine, 1984).

Robert Shellenberger and Judith Green, *From Ghost in the Box to Successful Biofeedback Training*, (Greely, Co.: Health Psychology Publications, 1986).

John Welwood, *Awakening the Heart: East-West Approaches to*

Psychotherapy and Healing Relationships (Boston: Shambhala, 1983).

Ken Wilber, Dan Brown and Jack Engler, *Transformations of Consciousness. Conventional and Contemplative Developmental Approaches,* (Boston: Shambhala, 1986).

AUDIO RECORDINGS

Catalogs of excellent and inexpensive meditation tapes are available from:

Hanuman Foundation Tape Library
P.O. Box 617498
Santa Cruz, Ca. 95061 USA

Dharma Seed Tape Library
P.O. Box 187
Northampton, Ma. 01060 USA

Audio recordings by the author of many of the methods in this book are available on cassettes and on a compact disk entitled *The Fine Art of Relaxation.* For more information contact your local bookseller or write to:

Wisdom Publications
23 Dering Street
London W1, England

Earth view Inc.
6514 18 Avenue Northeast
Seattle, Wa. 98115 USA

Publishers' note

We gratefully acknowledge the kind help of our well-wishers in Singapore who financed the production of this book.

Other Wisdom East-West Books

Radmila Moacanin
JUNG'S PSYCHOLOGY AND TIBETAN
BUDDHISM
Western and Eastern Paths to the Heart

In *Jung's Psychology and Tibetan Buddhism*
Radmila Moacanin reconciles an ancient
Eastern spiritual discipline with a
contemporary Western psychological system.
She touches on many of their major ideas and
methods and finds that, although there are
fundamental differences, both are vitally
concerned with what Jung called "the
tremendous experiment of becoming
conscious," successfully bridging the gap
between our deepest yearnings for spiritual
fulfilment and the demands of our mundane
life. Indeed, Western and Eastern paths to the
heart...

128pp, £6.95/$12.95

Other Wisdom East-West Books

Alan Keightley
INTO EVERY LIFE A LITTLE ZEN MUST
FALL
*A Christian Philosopher looks to Alan Watts
and the East*
Foreword by Professor John Hick

A committed and open hearted Christian, Alan
Keightley became inspired by the works of
Watts, Krishnamurti and the ideas of the East,
as well as the approaches of thinkers such as
Ludwig Wittgenstein, during his theological
and philosophical studies in the early
seventies.

From the standpoint of a Western Christian
he eloquently and with the conviction of
experience shows the need for each one of us to
break through the institutionalized, frozen idea
of religion and God-out-there, and to awaken
to the very real God within.

This is a marvellously refreshing book. It is a
clear example of the non-contradictory and
universal nature of all religions, and of the fact
that each has much to learn from the other.

194 pp, £6.95/$12.95

Other Wisdom East-West Books

Martin Willson
REBIRTH AND THE WESTERN
BUDDHIST

Belief in reincarnation is one of the greatest
cultural differences between Eastern and
Western thought. In this essay — published as
the first of a new series of Wisdom booklets —
Martin Willson presents arguments —
devotional, scriptural, observational, logical
and scientific — for and against rebirth. This
absorbing article is an excellent starting point,
with its more than one hundred references, for
Westerners interested in delving into this
controversial subject.

"...could make a significant impact on the
Western Buddhist world." FWBO Golden Drum

92pp, £3.25/$6.25

Other Wisdom East-West Books

BEYOND THERAPY
The Impact of Eastern Religions on
Psychological Theory and Practice
Edited by Guy Claxton

Buddhism and the spiritual/mystical traditions
in general have recently emerged as topics of
considerable interest to the general public and
also to those in the healing professions. Guy
Claxton, psychologist at University of London,
Chelsea College, has gathered together here
views from psychologists present at a recent
British Psychological Society symposium on
Buddhism and Psychology. The subject is the
impact of spiritual traditions on current
psychological thought.

Two areas are covered. Fisrt the theoretical is
examined; Buddhist ideas about self, identity
and personality and how these go beyond or
can be interpreted in terms of current
psychological concepts. Secondly, the
contributors look at the practical application
such as research on meditation, the value of
contemporary therapeutic techniques and the
question of spiritual development and personal
development.

352pp, £9.95/$18.95